Robert M. Sherfield • Patricia G. Moody

Cornerstones for Professionalism

Fourth Custom Edition for the University of South Carolina
HRSM 301

Taken from:
Cornerstones for Professionalism, Second Edition
by Robert M. Sherfield and Patricia G. Moody

Pearson Education, Inc., 330 Hudson Street, New York, New York 10013
A Pearson Education Company
www.pearsoned.com

Printed in the United States of America

1 17

000200010272101568

JC/AD

ISBN 10: 1-323-76608-1
ISBN 13: 978-1-323-76608-8

CORNERSTONES
FOR
PROFESSIONALISM

BRIEF CONTENTS

Taken from: *Cornerstones for Professionalism*, Second Edition
by Robert M. Sherfield and Patricia G. Moody

PART ONE: MANAGING YOU

1 DISCOVER 3
DISCOVERING WHO YOU ARE

2 PROSPER 29
UNDERSTANDING FINANCIAL INTELLIGENCE

PART TWO: MANAGING YOUR LIFE

3 BUILD 65
BUILDING YOUR PROFESSIONAL IMAGE

4 SOCIALIZE 85
PROFESSIONAL DRESS AND DINING WITH CLASS

5 CHANGE 97
DIRECTING YOUR LIFE THROUGH CONTINUOUS POSITIVE CHANGE

PART THREE: MANAGING YOUR CAREER

6 CONNECT 123
CREATING AND MAINTAINING A PROFESSIONAL NETWORK

7 PLAN 131
CREATING A DYNAMIC EMPLOYMENT PACKAGE AND JOB SEARCH PLAN

8 INTERVIEW 149
INTERVIEWING LIKE A PRO

9 PRIORITIZE 169
STRATEGIES FOR MANAGING PRIORITIES AND AVOIDING WORKPLACE LAND MINES

10 SERVE 205
MAXIMIZING CUSTOMER SERVICE AND PRODUCTIVITY IN THE WORKPLACE

CONTENTS

Taken from: *Cornerstones for Professionalism*, Second Edition
by Robert M. Sherfield and Patricia G. Moody

PART ONE: MANAGING YOU

chapter one
DISCOVER

DISCOVERING WHO YOU ARE   3

Capitalizing on Your Strengths   8
Identify Your Personality Type And
  Use It To Best Advantage   9
Understanding Personality Typing (Typology)   11
Why Personality Matters   12
How Personality Affects Career Choice   13
■ GRADUATE QUOTE   15
Know What You Want From Life and Work   15
True Colors   17

chapter two
PROSPER

UNDERSTANDING FINANCIAL
INTELLIGENCE   29

Taking Control of Your Money   31
Empower Yourself Through Wise Financial Decisions—
  Starting Now!   31
Take Time to Plan a Budget and Stick to It   32
■ POSITIVE HABITS AT WORK   34
What You Need to Know about Student Loans   35
■ GRADUATE QUOTE   36
Good Versus Bad Loans   38
The All-Important FICO Score   43
Making Wise Financial Decisions Beyond College
  Years   46
■ BIGGEST INTERVIEW BLUNDERS   46
■ REFLECTIONS: PUTTING IT ALL TOGETHER   49
■ DIGITAL BRIEFCASE   49
■ REFERENCES   53
Prosper   55

PART TWO: MANAGING YOUR LIFE

chapter three
BUILD

BUILDING YOUR PROFESSIONAL
IMAGE   65

Creating Your Own Personal Brand—Me, Inc.   67
The Power of Optimism and The Right Attitude   67
Getting Rid of Negativism and Avoiding Negative
  People   69
Choose Optimism and Surround Yourself with
  Optimistic People   70
■ POSITIVE HABITS AT WORK   70
■ BIGGEST INTERVIEW BLUNDERS   72
Understand Your Emotional Responses   72
Articulate Your Hopes and Goals   72
■ REFLECTIONS: PUTTING IT ALL TOGETHER   73
■ DIGITAL BRIEFCASE   73
■ REFERENCES   75
Personal Brand Inventory   77
Descriptive Words   79
LinkedIn Grading Rubric   81
Official College of HRSM Alumni LinkedIn
Network Access Form   83

chapter four
SOCIALIZE

PROFESSIONAL DRESS AND
DINING WITH CLASS   85

Perfect Your Professional Image   86
■ GRADUATE QUOTE   90
Dine with Class   92
■ REFERENCES   94
Professional Attire   95

chapter five
CHANGE
DIRECTING YOUR LIFE THROUGH
CONTINUOUS POSITIVE
CHANGE 97

You Are on Your Way 99
Accepting Change as A Natural Part of Life 100
Drivers, Dodgers, and Defeatists 100
Strategies for Dealing With Change 100
■ GRADUATE QUOTE 101
Skills and Abilities Valued By Employers 103
Cornerstones for Success in A Changing World 104
■ BIGGEST INTERVIEW BLUNDERS 107
Moving up the Ladder 107
Positive Habits at Work 108
Creating Multiple Revenue Streams 109
Downsizing, Rightsizing, RIFs, Terminations,
    Outsourcing, Layoffs 110
Designing A Career Plan 111
■ REFLECTIONS: PUTTING IT ALL TOGETHER 114
■ DIGITAL BRIEFCASE 114
■ REFERENCES 115
Life-Work-Balance Worksheet 117

PART THREE: MANAGING YOUR CAREER

chapter six
CONNECT
CREATING AND MAINTAINING
A PROFESSIONAL
NETWORK 123

Professionalism Defined 125
Setting Yourself Apart and Finding Your
    Direction 125
Networking 127
HRSM Alumni Society Career Night 129

chapter seven
PLAN
CREATING A DYNAMIC
EMPLOYMENT PACKAGE
AND JOB SEARCH PLAN 131

Overview of The Human Resources Department 133
Making an Important Choice 134
■ BIGGEST INTERVIEW BLUNDERS 135
Planning for the Future 136
Workin' 9 to 5—Or Trying To 137
Write a Powerful and Concise Cover Letter 138
■ POSITIVE HABITS AT WORK 140
Understand the Do's and Don'ts of Memorable
    Resumes 140
■ GRADUATE QUOTE 141
Building Your Resume 144
HRSM Resume Guide 145
Reference Document Guide 146
Job Search & Resume Workshop 147

chapter eight
INTERVIEW
INTERVIEWING LIKE
A PRO 149

The Big Day Is Here 151
Preparing for the Interview 152
Dressing for Success 155
Anticipating the Interviewer's Questions 155
■ GRADUATE QUOTE 157
■ BIGGEST INTERVIEW BLUNDERS 159
Ask Informed Questions 159
Rough, Tough, Hard Questions 159
■ POSITIVE HABITS AT WORK 161
Win, Lose, or Draw, Always Say Thank You
    in Writing 162
■ REFLECTIONS: PUTTING IT ALL TOGETHER 164
■ DIGITAL BRIEFCASE 164
■ REFERENCES 164
Behavioral Interviewing–the STAR Method 165
Behavioral Interviewing–Observation Feedback 167

chapter nine

PRIORITIZE

STRATEGIES FOR MANAGING
PRIORITIES AND AVOIDING
WORKPLACE LAND MINES 169

Time—You Have All There Is 171

Time Management and Self-Discipline 172

I'll Do It When I Have a Little Free Time 173

■ BIGGEST INTERVIEW BLUNDERS 174

Planning, Doodling, or Begging 174

Absolutely No . . . Well, Maybe 174

Beginning Your Day With Peace 176

The Dreaded "P" Word 177

■ POSITIVE HABITS AT WORK 178

Getting the Most Out of This Moment 179

Evaluating How You Spend Your Time 181

■ GRADUATE QUOTE 182

Eliminating Distractions and Interruptions 185

Planning and Preparing 186

Navigating Land Mines 190

"Water Cooler" Gossip Groups 190

■ POSITIVE HABITS AT WORK 190

■ BIGGEST INTERVIEW BLUNDERS 191

Workplace Romances 193

Don't Party at the Company Party 194

Alcohol and Substance Abuse 196

HRSM 301 Class Activity 199

chapter ten

SERVE

MAXIMIZING CUSTOMER SERVICE
AND PRODUCTIVITY IN THE
WORKPLACE 205

The Importance of Customer Service 207

■ GRADUATE QUOTE 209

Dealing with Difficult Customers 212

■ BIGGEST INTERVIEW BLUNDERS 213

Customer Service for Electronic and Mobile
   Commerce 214

■ REFLECTIONS: PUTTING IT ALL TOGETHER 215

■ DIGITAL BRIEFCASE 215

■ REFERENCES 216

HRSM 301 Practical Exam 217

Welcome!

All of us at the College of Hospitality, Retail, and Sport Management are excited that you will be a part of the Marnie Pearce Professional Development seminar this semester. We appreciate your hard work and dedication to all of your classes, and we sincerely hope you will find this seminar an investment that pays back many times over in the months and years ahead.

The goal of this seminar is to equip each of our graduates with the skills to design a comprehensive plan to pursue and achieve your professional career goals in the hospitality, retail, sport, entertainment, and technology industries. We will focus, however, on proven strategies that are adaptable to any organization regardless of industry.

Once again, welcome. Thank you for all that you do as a student in the College of HRSM by representing the University of South Carolina through your class involvement, internships, and future careers! We wish you nothing but success in all that you pursue!

Sincerely,

Hamoon Oh
Dean - HRSM

College of HRSM Professionalism Certification

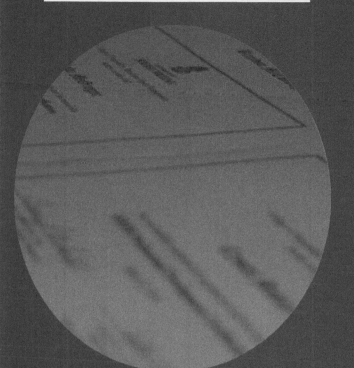

Each student who successfully completes all designated instruction and evaluation components of the professionalism seminar listed below will be awarded the College of Hospitality, Retail and Sport Management *Professionalism Certification.* This certification will include the following areas:

- [ ] Personality/Temperament Training
- [ ] Accomplishment Based Resume
- [ ] Salary Negotiation
- [ ] Networking
- [ ] Interviewing
- [ ] Professional Attire
- [ ] Diversity in the Workplace
- [ ] Personal Branding
- [ ] Professional Online Presence
- [ ] Life-Work Balance
- [ ] Workplace Landmines
- [ ] Business Dining Etiquette
- [ ] Customer Service

Successful completion of each component of the certification requires full participation in each component listed above. Students who do not attend class sessions when a particular area of the certification is covered will not be awarded the professionalism certification by the College of HRSM. This certification is independent of your grade in the seminar.

UNIVERSITY OF
SOUTH CAROLINA
College of Hospitality, Retail and Sport Management

Conversation Activity

The Marnie Pearce Professionalism Program

UNIVERSITY OF
SOUTH CAROLINA
College of Hospitality, Retail
and Sport Management

1. Identify personal characteristics to effectively interact with internal and external environments.
5. Identify potential questions and concerns for future interview situations.
6. Develop effective communication skills, verbal and non-verbal, for the workplace.
9. Develop strategies for effective networking and mentoring.
10. Participate in professional development activities that ensure a smooth transition into the workplace.

Conversation Activity— This is always loud and full of energy. It will seem like organized chaos!

- Fill out each of your 7 cards

- Save 1 of your cards!! Don't give it away!
- HOW THIS WILL WORK: You only have a short amount of time to meet as many people as you can from our class. The goal is to meet at least 6 new people. Let's see if you can meet more.

When you are prompted to do so, pair off with someone you don't know, give each partner a moment to introduce themselves, then take a minute to ask each other a few questions. Suggestions for discussion are: **So tell me about yourself!** Then give a short explanation of yourself (insert elevator speech!) and try to be interesting. Please be interested in the other person and not just yourself. Take notes. Be a good listener. Have fun with this! Slip your new network connection a card with your name and email address! Follow up and stay connected.

Questions: What are your career goals/aspirations? What is your area of expertise? What has been your biggest success so far?

Printed Name_____

PART ONE:
MANAGING YOU

chapter one

DISCOVER

DISCOVERING WHO YOU ARE

Believe you can and you are halfway there.
—Theodore Roosevelt

Figure 1.1 Solving the "Me Puzzle"

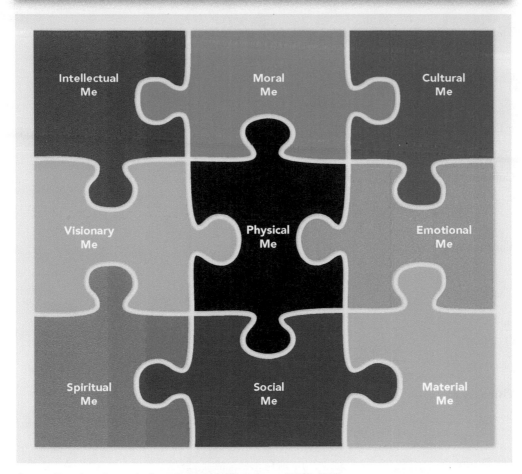

Source: Based on the work of psychologist William James (1842–1910).

Challenge: I sometimes judge others too harshly when they do not have the same work ethic that I possess. This can become a problem when I move up the ladder and begin supervising people.

Overcome: I plan to begin listening more and to try to understand others' backgrounds and problems before making judgments.

Intellectual Me

Strength: _____

_____

The Future: _____

_____

Challenge: _____

_____

Overcome: _____

_____

Moral Me

Strength: _____

_____

The Future: _____

_____

Challenge: _____

_____

Overcome: _____

_____

Cultural Me

Strength: _____

_____

The Future: _____

_____

Challenge: _____

_____

Overcome: _____

_____

Visionary Me

Strength: _____

_____

The Future: _____

_____

Challenge: _____

_____

Overcome: _____

_____

Physical Me

Strength: _____

_____

The Future: _____

_____

Challenge: _____

_____

Overcome: _____

_____

Emotional Me

Strength: _____

_____

The Future: _____

_____

Challenge: _____

_____

Overcome: _____

_____

Spiritual Me

Strength: _____

_____

The Future: _____

_____

Challenge: _____

_____

Overcome: _____

_____

Social Me

Strength: _____

_____

The Future: _____

_____

Challenge: _____

_____

Overcome: _____

_____

Material Me

Strength: _____

_____

The Future: _____

_____

Challenge: _____

_____

Overcome: _____

_____

Spiritual Me	**Social Me**	**Material Me**
What I believe	My relationships	What I have
My religion	My activities	What I want
Wisdom gained	My associations	What I need to survive
Meditation	My social involvement	Economic background
Altruistic notions		
My "grounding"		
Intellectual Me	**Moral Me**	**Cultural Me**
What I know	Character	How I interact with others
Common sense	Ethics/Values	Knowledge of my own culture, norms, heritage, environment, race, etc.
Skills I possess	Choices and decisions	
Critical thinking	Reactions	
Reasoning	Principles	
Problem solving		
Visionary Me	**Physical Me**	**Emotional Me**
Where I am going	My health	What I feel
My goals and dreams for the future	My appearance and grooming	How am I guided by emotions
What skills I need to be successful	My body	My heart vs. my head
	My habits	How I manage conflicts and challenges

CAPITALIZING ON YOUR STRENGTHS

What Do You Have Going for You?

Study the following statements carefully:

"I am super organized."

"I am extremely good at my profession."

"I know I can solve that problem."

"I can't find a thing on this desk."

"I feel so stupid at work."

"I don't even know where to begin."

Do you capitalize on all your strengths at work?

Shutterstock

Notice the difference between these perspectives? One person seems optimistic and appears to know his or her abilities and strengths, and the other is unsure, timid, and pessimistic. Who would you hire? Who would you like working on your team? Knowing what you're good at and owning those strengths can be an enormously positive attribute and can give you another competitive asset to highlight on your resumé. Basically, the question that must be answered is, "What do I have going for me?" If you don't know your strengths, it will be impossible to convey them to an employer. It is also impossible to use the strengths that you don't even know you have.

Perhaps you've never thought of yourself as a problem solver, but think again. Don't you do this on a daily basis with your personal budget? Your children? Your studies? Juggling schedules with work and classes? Making your iPad or smartphone work properly? You solve problems every day, and acknowledging these skills can only make it stronger.

You probably have strengths that you have never thoroughly identified. Take your time and consider the following list of traits and abilities. Circle your strengths and add any that are not listed. Be honest with yourself because you will return to this list later.

Accountable	Budget-minded	Organized
Positive attitude	Intuitive	Stable
Punctual	Inquisitive	Rational
Ethical	Reliable	Tolerant
Resourceful	Humorous	Compassionate
Hopeful	Self-reliant	Decisive
Courageous	Competent	Grateful
Loyal	Sincere	Open-minded
Stylish	Helpful	Friendly
Optimistic	Respectful	Trusting
Well-groomed	Neat	Prepared
Supportive	Honest	Strong
Reserved	Logical	Spiritual
Warm	Versatile	Motivated
Grounded	Trustworthy	Creative
Modest	Imaginative	Fair
Flexible	Persuasive	Analytical
Loving	Yielding	Fun-loving
Forgiving	Articulate	Giving

_____   _____   _____

_____   _____   _____

_____   _____   _____

IDENTIFY YOUR PERSONALITY TYPE AND USE IT TO BEST ADVANTAGE

Understanding your personality type enables you to use your best assets to your advantage. Having the knowledge of different personality types also helps you better understand others. In Figure 1.2 you will be able to take the PAP, a personality profile assessment that is designed to help you understand your personality type.

Figure 1.2 Take the PAP

The Personality Assessment Profile

Directions: Read each statement carefully and thoroughly. After reading the statement, rate your response using the scale below. There are no right or wrong answers. This is not a timed survey. The PAP is based, in part, on the Myers-Briggs Type Indicator (MBTI) by Katharine Briggs and Isabel Briggs-Myers.

3 = Often Applies   2 = Sometimes Applies   1 = Never or Almost Never Applies

_____ 1a. I am a very talkative person.

_____ 1b. I am a more reflective person than a verbal person.

_____ 2a. I am a very factual and literal person.

_____ 2b. I look to the future and I can see possibilities.

_____ 3a. I value truth and justice over tact and emotion.

_____ 3b. I find it easy to empathize with other people.

_____ 4a. I am very ordered and efficient.

_____ 4b. I enjoy having freedom from control.

_____ 5a. I am a very friendly and social person.

_____ 5b. I enjoy listening to others more than talking.

_____ 6a. I enjoy being around and working with people who have a great deal of common sense.

_____ 6b. I enjoy being around and working with people who are dreamers and have a great deal of imagination.

_____ 7a. One of my motivating forces is to do a job very well.

_____ 7b. I like to be recognized for, and I am motivated by, my accomplishments and awards.

_____ 8a. I like to plan out my day before I go to bed.

_____ 8b. When I get up on a non-school or non-work day, I just like to let the day "plan itself."

_____ 9a. I like to express my feelings and thoughts.

_____ 9b. I enjoy a great deal of tranquility and quiet time to myself.

_____ 10a. I am a very pragmatic and realistic person.

_____ 10b. I like to create new ideas, methods, or ways of doing things.

_____ 11a. I make decisions with my brain.

_____ 11b. I make decisions with my heart.

_____ 12a. I am a very disciplined and orderly person.

_____ 12b. I don't make a lot of plans.

_____ 13a. I like to work with a group of people.

_____ 13b. I would rather work independently.

_____ 14a. I learn best if I can see it, touch it, smell it, taste it, or hear it.

_____ 14b. I learn best by relying on my gut feelings or intuition.

_____ 15a. I am quick to criticize others.

_____ 15b. I compliment others very easily and quickly.

_____ 16a. My life is systematic and organized.

_____ 16b. I don't really pay attention to deadlines.

_____ 17a. I can be myself when I am around others.

_____ 17b. I can be myself when I am alone.

_____ 18a. I live in the here and now, in the present.

_____ 18b. I live in the future, planning and dreaming.

_____ 19a. I think that if someone breaks the rules, the person should be punished.

_____ 19b. I think that if someone breaks the rules, we should look at the person who broke the rules, examine the rules, and look at the situation at hand before a decision is made.

_____ 20a. I do my work, then I play.

_____ 20b I play, then do my work.

Refer to your score on each individual question. Place that score beside the appropriate question number below. Then, tally each line at the side.

Score					Total Across	Code
1a ____	5a ____	9a ____	13a ____	17a ____	____	E Extrovert
1b ____	5b ____	9b ____	13b ____	17b ____	____	I Introvert
2a ____	6a ____	10a ____	14a ____	18a ____	____	S Sensing
2b ____	6b ____	10b ____	14b ____	18b ____	____	N Intuition
3a ____	7a ____	11a ____	15a ____	19a ____	____	T Thinking
3b ____	7b ____	11b ____	15b ____	19b ____	____	F Feeling
4a ____	8a ____	12a ____	16a ____	20a ____	____	J Judging
4b ____	8b ____	12b ____	16b ____	20b ____	____	P Perceiving

PAP Scores
Personality Indicator

Look at the scores on your PAP. Is your score higher in the E or I line? Is your score higher in the S or N line? Is your score higher in the T or F line? Is your score higher in the J or P line? Write the code to the side of each section below.

Is your higher score	E or I	Code	_____
Is your higher score	S or N	Code	_____
Is your higher score	T or F	Code	_____
Is your higher score	J or P	Code	_____

Source: © Robert M. Sherfield, Ph.D.

UNDERSTANDING PERSONALITY TYPING (TYPOLOGY)

What Do These Letters Mean to Me?

The questions on the PAP helped you discover whether you are extroverted or introverted (E or I), sensing or intuitive (S or N), thinking or feeling (T or F), and judging or perceiving (J or P). These questions were based, in part, on work done by Carl Jung, Katharine Briggs, and Isabel Briggs-Myers.

In 1921, Swiss psychologist Carl Jung (1875–1961) published his work *Psychological Types.* In this book, Jung suggested that human behavior is not random. He felt that behavior follows patterns, and these patterns are caused by differences in the way people use their minds. In 1942, Isabel Briggs-Myers and her mother, Katharine Briggs, began to put Jung's theory into practice. They developed the Myers-Briggs Type Indicator, which after more than 50 years of research and refinement has become the most widely used instrument for identifying and studying personality.

Please keep in mind that no part of this assessment measures your worth, your success factors, how smart you are, or your value as a human being. The questions on the PAP assisted you in identifying your type, but we do not want you to assume that one personality type is better or worse, more or less valuable, or more or less likely to be successful. What personality typing can do is to "help us discover what best motivates and energizes each of us as individuals" (Tieger & Barron-Tieger, 2001).

WHY PERSONALITY MATTERS

What Does My Personality Type Say about Me?

When all of the combinations of E/I, S/N, T/F, and J/P are combined, there are 16 personality types. Everyone will fit into one of the following categories:

ISTJ	ISFJ	INFJ	INTJ
ISTP	ISFP	INFP	INTP
ESTP	ESFP	ENFP	ENTP
ESTJ	ESFJ	ENFJ	ENTJ

Let's take a look at the four major categories of typing. Notice that the higher your score in one area, the stronger your personality type is for that area. For instance, if you scored 15 on the E (extroversion) questions, this means that you are a strong extrovert. If you scored 15 on the I (introversion) questions, this means that you are a strong introvert. However, if you scored 7 on the E questions and 8 on the I questions, your score indicates that you possess almost the same amount of extroverted and introverted qualities. The same is true for every category on the PAP.

E Versus I (Extroversion/Introversion)

This category deals with the way we interact with others and the world around us.

Extroverts prefer to live in the outside world, drawing their strength from other people. They are outgoing and love interaction. They usually make decisions with others in mind. They enjoy being the center of attention. There are usually few secrets about extroverts.

Introverts draw their strength from the inner world. They need to spend time alone to think and ponder. They are usually quiet and reflective. They usually make decisions by themselves. They do not like being the center of attention. They are private.

S Versus N (Sensing/Intuition)

This category deals with the way we learn and deal with information.

Sensing types gather information through their five senses. They have a hard time believing something if it cannot be seen, touched, smelled, tasted, or heard. They like concrete facts and details. They do not rely on intuition or gut feelings. They usually have a great deal of common sense.

Intuitive types are not very detail-oriented. They can see possibilities, and they rely on their gut feelings. Usually, they are very innovative people. They tend to live in the future and often get bored once they have mastered a task.

T Versus F (Thinking/Feeling)

This category deals with the way we make decisions.

Thinkers are very logical people. They do not make decisions based on feelings or emotion. They are analytical and sometimes do not take others' values into consideration when making decisions. They can easily identify the flaws of others. They can be seen as insensitive and lacking compassion.

Feelers make decisions based on what they feel is right and just. They like to have harmony, and they value others' opinions and feelings. They are usually very tactful people who like to please others. They are very warm people.

J Versus P (Judging/Perceiving)

This category deals with the way we live.

Judgers are very orderly people. They must have a great deal of structure in their lives. They are good at setting goals and sticking to their goals. They are the type of people who would seldom, if ever, play before their work was completed.

Perceivers are just the opposite. They are less structured and more spontaneous. They do not like timelines. Unlike the judger, they will play before their work is done. They will take every chance to delay a decision or judgment. Sometimes, they can become involved in too many things at one time.

HOW PERSONALITY AFFECTS CAREER CHOICE

What Do I Want to Be When I Grow Up?

Taking personality and career tests and using them to help you decide which career you want to pursue is somewhat like playing the childhood game of "What Do I Want to Be When I Grow Up?" When taking career and personality tests, you need to remember that the results are indicators that will help you narrow the choices related to your personality, skills, and abilities; tests won't provide you with a specific career choice. Tests cannot pinpoint exactly what career you should pursue, but they can provide additional information to help you find your way. There are many free personality/career tests online and others you can access for a fee. To locate sites that will provide additional information related to personality types and career choices, use your Internet browser and type in keywords such as "careers for different personality types." Figure 1.3 provides suggestions of the types of careers that are best for specific personality types.

Figure 1.3   A Closer Look at Your Personality Type

Type	Attributes	Possible Careers
ISTJ—The Dutiful (7–10% of Americans)	Have great power of concentration; very serious; dependable; logical and realistic; take responsibility for their own actions; not easily distracted.	Accountant, purchasing agent, real estate, IRS agent, corrections officer, investment counselor, law researcher, technical writer, judge, mechanic
ISTP—The Mechanic (4–7% of Americans)	Very reserved; good at making things clear to others; interested in how and why things work; like to work with their hands; can sometimes be misunderstood as idle.	Police officer, intelligence officer, firefighter, athletic coach, engineer, technical trainer, logistic manager, EMT, surgical technician, banker, office manager, carpenter, landscape architect
ISFJ—The Nurturer (7–10% of Americans)	Hard workers; detail-oriented; considerate of others' feelings; friendly and warm to others; very conscientious; down-to-earth and like to be around the same.	Dentist, physician, biologist, surgical technician, teacher, speech pathologist, historian, clerical, bookkeeper, electrician, retail owner, counselor
ISFP—The Artist (5–7% of Americans)	Very sensitive and modest; adapt easily to change; they are respectful of others' feelings and values; take criticism personally; don't enjoy leadership roles.	Artist, chef, musician, nurse, medical assistant, surgeon, botanist, zoologist, science teacher, travel agent, game warden, coach, bookkeeper, clerical, insurance examiner
INFJ—The Protector (2–3% of Americans)	Enjoy an atmosphere where all get along; do what is needed of them; have strong beliefs and principles; enjoy helping others achieve their goals.	Career counselor, psychologist, teacher, social worker, clergy, artist, novelist, filmmaker, health care provider, human resource manager, agent, coach, crisis manager, mediator

(continued)

Figure 1.3 A Closer Look at Your Personality Type (continued)

Type	Attributes	Possible Careers
INFP—The Idealist (3–4% of Americans)	Work well alone; must know others well to interact; faithful to others and their jobs; excellent at communication; open-minded; dreamers; tend to do too much.	Entertainer, artist, editor, musician, professor, researcher, counselor, consultant, clergy, dietitian, massage therapist, human resources manager, events manager, corporate leader
INTJ—The Scientist (2–3% of Americans)	Very independent; enjoy challenges; inventors; can be skeptical; perfectionists; believe in their own work, sometimes to a fault.	Economist, financial planner, banker, budget analyst, scientist, astronomer, network specialist, computer programmer, engineer, curriculum designer, coroner, pathologist, attorney, manager
INTP—The Thinker (3–4% of Americans)	Extremely logical; very analytical; good at planning; love to learn; excellent problem solvers; don't enjoy needless conversation; hard to understand at times.	Software designer, programmer, systems analyst, network administrator, surgeon, veterinarian, lawyer, economist, architect, physicist, mathematician, college professor, writer, agent, producer
ESTP—The Doer (6–8% of Americans)	Usually very happy; don't let trivial things upset them; have very good memories; very good at working with things and taking them apart.	Police officer, firefighter, detective, military, investigator, paramedic, banker, investor, promoter, carpenter, chef, real estate broker, retail sales, insurance claims
ESTJ—The Guardian (12–15% of Americans)	"Take charge" people; like to get things done; focus on results; very good at organizing; good at seeing what will not work; responsible; realists.	Insurance agent, military, security, coach, credit analyst, project manager, auditor, general contractor, paralegal, stockbroker, executive, information officer, lawyer, controller, accounts manager
ESFP—The Performer (8–10% of Americans)	Very good at sports and active exercises; good common sense; easygoing; good at communication; can be impulsive; do not enjoy working alone; have fun and enjoy living and life.	Nurse, social worker, physician assistant, nutritionist, therapist, photographer, musician, film producer, social events coordinator, news anchor, fund raiser, host, retail sales
ESFJ—The Caregiver (11–14% of Americans)	Enjoy many friendly relationships; popular; love to help others; do not take criticism very well; need praise; need to work with people; organized; talkative; active.	Medical assistant, physician, nurse, teacher, coach, principal, social worker, counselor, clergy, court reporter, office manager, loan officer, public relations, customer service, caterer, office manager
ENFP—The Inspirer (6–7% of Americans)	Creative and industrious; can easily find success in activities and projects that interest them; good at motivating others; organized; do not like routine.	Journalist, writer, actor, newscaster, artist, director, public relations, teacher, clergy, psychologist, guidance counselor, trainer, project manager, human resources manager
ENFJ—The Giver (3–5% of Americans)	Very concerned about others' feelings; respect others; good leaders; usually popular; good at public speaking; can make decisions too quickly; trust easily.	Journalist, entertainer, TV producer, politician, counselor, clergy, psychologist, teacher, social worker, health care provider, customer service manager
ENTP—The Visionary (4–6% of Americans)	Great problem solvers; love to argue either side; can do almost anything; good at speaking/motivating; love challenges; very creative; do not like routine; overconfident.	Entrepreneur, manager, agent, journalist, attorney, urban planner, analyst, creative director, public relations, marketing, broadcaster, network solutions, politician, detective
ENTJ—The Executive (3–5% of Americans)	Excellent leaders; speak very well; hardworking; may be workaholics; may not give enough praise; like to learn; great planners; enjoy helping others reach their goals.	Executive, senior manager, administrator, consultant, editor, producer, financial planner, stockbroker, program designer, attorney, psychologist, engineer, network administrator

GRADUATE *Quote*

Nancy Kirkess
Graduate!
Empire College, Santa Rosa, CA
**Career: Concierge, River Rock Casino Visitors
and Convention Center**

As I was investigating and applying for employment during this stage in my life, I found that my criteria for the perfect job had changed from when I was younger.

I realized that an environment of mutual respect, where value and a sense of dignity were given to coworkers as well as clients, had risen to the top of my list.

KNOW WHAT YOU WANT FROM LIFE AND WORK

Are You Prepared to Go Get What You Want?

Some of the strongest, most dedicated people in the world struggle in their work and personal lives. Why? Because they have never really thought about what they want out of life or from their careers. They have never done the work required to answer this question—and it is work. What is it that you really want and need to be happy, fulfilled, and successful? What is the main thing that you really need to focus on? You may have never thought about the questions below, but consider them as you try to formulate an answer to the question, "What do I want from my life and my work?"

- Is my success tied to the amount of money I make?
- Are my friends and family more important than my career?
- What would I be willing to do to get ahead?
- What can I contribute to the world through my career?
- What really makes me happy? Will my career choice give this to me?
- Does my career choice suit my genuine interests?
- Does my current career choice really motivate me?
- Am I working toward this career for convenience or passion?
- Would I rather work inside or outside?
- Am I more of a leader or a follower?
- Do I want to travel with my work?
- Am I truly grounded in my ethics?
- Am I focused on the things that are life changing?

There is an old quote that says, "If you don't know where you're going, it doesn't matter which path you take." Many people have found this to be true in their personal and professional lives. Knowing what you want and need from your career and your life will be ultimately important to your happiness and success.

Delaney

True Colors

Opening Skit

Directions: Listen and watch as the skit is performed. Look for the colors (Orange, Gold, Blue, and Green) and listen to what is being said. Write two or three words that you believe describes each color.

<u>Blue</u>

-
-
-

<u>Gold</u>

-
-
-

<u>Green</u>

-
-
-

<u>Orange</u>

-
-
-

Reprinted by permission of True Colors International.

orange	gold	green	blue
③	②	①	④
①	④	②	③
①	④	②	③
①	④	②	③
①	④	②	②
③	④	①	②
10	**22**	**11**	**17**

① gold
② blue
③ green
④ orange

True Colors

Card Sort. Most like you to least like you (by picture) Blue Green Orange Gold

__4__ __1__ __3__ __2__

Card Sort. Most like you to least like you (by words) Blue Green Orange Gold

__3__ __1__ __2__ __4__

Scoring: Blue __17__ Green __11__ Orange __10__ Gold __22__

"There are no bad colors or color spectrums, so please, no color __bashing__."

Blue Attributes:

mediators, optimism, peace-makers, people pleasing, cooperation

Core needs and values of Blue are __relationships__.

Green Attributes: overall mood: cool, calm, collected

Core needs and values of Green are __Knowledge__.

Gold Attributes: overall mood: concerned

being prepared, loving the plan, loyal, rule followers, structure

Core needs and values of Gold are_____.

Orange Attributes:

testing limits   overall mood: excitement

Core needs and values of Orange are_____.

flexible lifestyle

Your Name (Printed): __Delaney Wood__

UNIVERSITY OF
SOUTH CAROLINA
College of Hospitality, Retail
and Sport Management

Brightening Activity

GOAL:

To better understand yourself and learn about others.

1) Break into groups of brightest color. Once you have a complete table, select a table leader to record comments and ideas.

2) PROCESS: In your color groups discuss:

What are your strengths, joys, values and needs.

leadership ←

Strengths
- organized (planning)
- stable
- dependable & responsible

Values
- loyalty
- family
- tradition

Joys
- caring   success
- helpful   structure
- affection

Needs
- accomplish goals
- structure
- clarity
- routine & organization

22

17

11

10

What are your stressors and frustrations?

Stressors
- messes (people who are)
- procrastinating (time management)
- change
- being late (time management)
- lack of planning
- unreliability (in people)

Frustrations
- unable to stay on task (others)
- not meeting standards
- irresponsible & immature (others)
- disrespect (others)
- not accomplishing

3) Report Out.

don't:
be messy, sloppy, off task, late, too go with the flow

Table Color: __gold__

UNIVERSITY OF
SOUTH CAROLINA
College of Hospitality, Retail
and Sport Management

21

Brightening Activity

GOAL

To better understand yourself and how to treat others.

1) Break into groups of three (3) or four (4). You have a complete printed reference table. Read it as reference material and discuss.

3) PROCESS: Score your answer appropriately.

What are some strengths, joys, values and needs.

organized (planning)
stable
dependable & responsible

caring — success
helpful — structure
affection

loyalty
family
tradition

accomplish goals
structure
clarity
routine & organization

bosses (people who are)
structured (time management)
change
being late (time management)
lack of planning
unreliability (in people)

unable to stay on task (others)
not meeting standards
irresponsible & immature (others)
disrespect (others)
not disciplining

so many sloppy off tasks, lets too go with the flow
old

True Colors Assessment Grading Rubric

Assignment: The goal of this assignment is to ensure that you have a useful understanding of how True Colors can be applied and serve as a resource for you in work and life. Conduct the True Colors assessment on a parent, roommate, significant other, spouse, co-worker, or boss. Create a brief presentation (Prezi, YouTube, Pecha Kucha, PowerPoint, etc.) that answers the following questions, based on your new found understanding of your color spectrum and theirs.

    1) Describes the results of the True Colors Assessment for you and them.

        2) What are their needs and values?

    3) How might their perception of me be different than how I see myself?

    4) What might describe the best workplace environment for them?

Please don't ask them to answer these questions outright, let's see if we can come up with accurate results. Keep the word count to a minimum by making the presentation creative!

    As a guide, the presentation should last no more than 2-3 minutes.

	10 Unsatisfactory	15 Satisfactory	18 Proficient	20 Exemplary
Created a brief presentation (Prezi, YouTube, Pecha Kucha, PowerPoint, etc.) that was creative and original.				
1) Describes the results of the True Colors Assessment for you and them.				
2) What are their needs and values?				
3) How might their perception of me be different than how I see myself?				
4) What might describe the best workplace environment for them?				

UNIVERSITY OF
SOUTH CAROLINA

College of Hospitality, Retail and Sport Management

Quick Look at Reframing in True Colors

Blue

You may see yourself as. . .	Others may see you as. . .
A people pleaser	Too giving
A very good communicator	Talking too much
Empathetic	Overly sensitive
Caring	Too trusting
Romantic	Too tender

Green

mentally tough

You may see yourself as. . .	Others may see you as. . .
Secure in yourself	Arrogant
One who enjoys his/her own company	Self-centered
Being profound	Academically demanding
Visionary	Absent minded
Logical	Insensitive

→ afraid to open up

• don't like to be pushed
• like time
• logic

Gold

You may see yourself as. . .	Others may see you as. . .
Organized	Rigid —
Dependable	Too conventional
Firm	Resistant to change —
Practical, Down-to-Earth	Boring
Providing structure	Too serious —

→ controlling uptight bossy judgy (blue) too opinionated resistant

stress: people who don't stay on task, unreliable, immature, when we don't meet standards

Orange

You may see yourself as. . .	Others may see you as. . .
Easy-going —	Irresponsible *no plan*
Fun-loving —	Immature
Open to change —	Unable to stay on task
One who enjoys life	Obnoxious, annoying
Independent	Self-centered

→ untrust-worthy unnessecary risks

• high energy fun adventures
• like tangible rewards
• stressers: control, organized, structure, rules, school, future, pending obligations, deadlines

orange & gold = opposites

chapter two

PROSPER

UNDERSTANDING
FINANCIAL INTELLIGENCE

It's good to have money and the things money can buy,
but it's good, too, to check up once in a while and make
sure you haven't lost the things that money can't buy.

—George Lorimer

TAKING CONTROL OF YOUR MONEY

How Can You Manage Your Money Wisely?

Exactly what is personal financial management? Quite simply, it is understanding the process of taking control of your income and expenses and managing them to maximize your assets. Income is the money that you have coming in—it might be from work, loans, parents, or gifts. An expense is anything that you are spending money on—this includes items such as rent, car payment, utilities, bills, eating out, and the like.

Many, if not most, college students have had few lessons in personal financial management when they begin their college careers. In some cases, parents have always just handed over money when students asked for it or needed it. Most students are ill-prepared to make good financial management decisions. Unfortunately, many students get themselves in serious financial trouble simply because they don't know any better. If you want to learn to make wise decisions about how to save, spend, and invest your money, you can do it. Learning to manage money is one of the most valuable lessons you will ever have, and it is certainly one that you will want to take with you as you begin your career!

The importance of managing your personal finances well cannot be overemphasized, regardless of what profession you enter. For the first time, you may become aware of the importance of maintaining a good credit score, the significance of your credit card debt, and how difficult it can be to repay college loans. You will begin to realize how expensive taxes and other deductions are to your take-home pay. The good news is that you can learn to manage your money well and still have many of the things you want and need.

iStockphoto

How many credit cards do you currently have? Do you use them wisely?

> Don't tell me where your priorities are. Show me where you spend your money, and I will tell you what they are.
> —James W. Frick

EMPOWER YOURSELF THROUGH WISE FINANCIAL DECISIONS—STARTING NOW!

What Goals Do I Need to Set for Financial Success?

Discipline is extremely important to your financial success because it is much easier to spend than to save and much more instantly gratifying to eat out, purchase clothes, or travel now than to struggle to save 10 percent or more of your income. If you can focus on the following, however, it might help you develop more discipline: If you save now and invest wisely, the time will come when you can have almost anything you want! You can retire early and travel; you can educate your children; you can live in a nice home and drive luxury cars; you can spend money without worrying about every dime; you can give generously to your favorite charity. Delayed

> *I've been rich and I've been poor. Rich is better.*
> —Sophie Tucker

gratification is the first key. This means that you delay spending money on things that give you instant pleasure and wait until you can afford them. Starting early is the second step to developing financial discipline.

If you earn the typical starting salary and are totally on your own, you will find that you can't buy everything you would like. Before you rush out and buy a new car or a new wardrobe, give yourself time to understand your total financial picture to avoid making huge mistakes that are not easily resolved. You've waited this long; be patient a little longer until you have had time to evaluate your income, debts, and other financial obligations. If you have never had to manage a budget, financial management may be more difficult than you imagined. You need to keep in mind that you have to be able to pay household expenses, taxes, insurance, medical bills—on and on the list goes. And many students must begin repaying student loans soon after graduation.

In the space below, list the things you purchase on a daily basis that are wants rather than needs. (An example might be a grande size latte that you *"must"* have every morning that costs $3.95. Oh, and a muffin to go with it for $3.50 is nice, too.)

_____

_____

_____

TOTAL $ _____

List three strategies that you can use—starting tomorrow—to avoid these spending behaviors.

_____

_____

_____

TAKE TIME TO PLAN A BUDGET AND STICK TO IT

How Will I Ever Pay All These Bills?

Most people do not budget. Some have a reasonable idea of what they can spend and how much they require to make the house payment, car payment, food, utilities, and the like, but it is just a guess; others just "go with the flow" and spend until they run out of money and then use plastic. Needless to say, people who do not budget their money and plan carefully rarely ever accumulate much. They are the people who are pushing 70 and older and cannot afford to retire. They have never sat down and decided to live within their income and use their money wisely, nor have they really determined exactly where their money is being spent. As a result, they are often strapped for money, late with payments, and have little or no savings and investments. In this section, we want to help you understand how to go about creating a spending/savings budget. Our goal is to help you become financially intelligent, be able to provide for yourself, become wise about spending, saving, and investing money, and be able to retire comfortably. Budgeting is the first step!

> *The only way not to think about money is to have a great deal of it.*
> —Edith Wharton

Many people do not use their discretionary income wisely. Discretionary income is the money you have left after paying all your expenses. This is the difference in being financially secure and being broke. The information in this chapter is intended to help you make wise decisions about how you spend your money and to instill in you the belief that money management is an everyday process. If you are going to be financially secure, you cannot afford to live day-to-day and hand-to-mouth with no plan for accumulating wealth.

An exercise follows that is designed to help you prepare to manage your money and make wise decisions by using a budget. A budget is an itemized summary of how you plan to spend your financial resources during a specified period of time. By working from a budget, you will be able to pinpoint exactly what your money wasters are and determine how to manage your money more wisely. Money wasters are items on which you spend money that you could have easily done without—for example, a daily grande latte and a muffin that might cost you as much as $8.50 or more.

One very important item on your budget is savings. The best way to save money is to have this money automatically deducted before you ever touch it. You may think you cannot possibly save money, but experts say that you need at least six months' salary in reserve for unexpected emergencies. You will need to discipline yourself to save monthly for items that may come due only once or twice a year, such as car insurance or taxes. In addition, your savings can be used to help you buy a house or replace an old car. If you have children, you will need to save for their education expenses.

Before beginning this exercise, study the following financial tips for new college graduates (Fowles, 2011).

- Pick your job carefully. Select a job you can really enjoy even if it pays less than another one that you might hate.

- Don't live with your parents. You'll receive conflicting advice about this, but you should not move in with your parents if you are going to spend your money on entertainment, new cars, trips, and the like. If you do this, you are not growing or learning to take responsibility for yourself. If, however, you have overwhelming student loans and you will use this opportunity to double up on paying off loans, it's not a bad idea.

- Buy a used car. You can buy a preowned car that looks new but costs a lot less than a new one. The higher your car payments, the more difficulty you may have qualifying for a mortgage loan. Your insurance will also be cheaper.

- Make budgeting a habit. Budgeting can be like dieting. After a few months, it is easy to drift back into bad habits. Construct a carefully planned budget and stick to it!

- Learn about personal finance. There are so many good, easy-to-understand books about personal finance. Read, read, read because you can never know too much about managing your money, saving for big purchases, and planning for retirement. (Fowles, 2011)

Using these tips, along with the following information, answer the questions regarding your personal budget.

In this scenario, we will assume that you live alone, that you make $35,000 a year, and that you are contributing 10 percent to your company's tax-deferred profit-sharing program so you will be taxed on only $31,500. (*Tax deferred* means that you don't pay taxes on income until you withdraw it later in retirement.) Let's also assume that you have company benefits that provide you full coverage for your personal health insurance and 1.5 times your salary in life insurance so you don't have to spend any of your salary on those items. If you are married and have children and cover them under your health insurance, this amount will be deducted from your take-home pay. Providing fewer benefits is the trend in many companies. When you consider a new job, find out about benefits that are provided for you. Benefits include health insurance, life insurance, dental insurance, profit-sharing programs, free parking, child care facilities, exercise facilities, and others. Benefits that are provided by your company are better than money in your pocket in some cases and may offset a lower salary and actually be a better deal for you, especially if the company pays the entire amount.

First, let's differentiate between **fixed** and **variable expenses.** Fixed expenses remain the same and are items such as rent, car payment, and student loan payments. Variable expenses change each month and include utilities, food, medical expenses, and miscellaneous. Budget for variable expenses by making your best estimate.

For purposes of this exercise, let's assume that you are in the 28 percent federal income tax bracket and that you live in a state that has a 7 percent state income tax. This means that

POSITIVE HABITS *at Work*

Talk to a human resource specialist about any benefits that you do not fully understand before making a decision to enroll in specific options. You should ask questions until you know enough to make wise decisions. The worst thing you can do is to make no decision. Your future depends on your retirement decisions! If your company has a pension plan or a 401(k), learn everything you can about it and enroll as soon as possible.

35 percent of your salary ($11,025) will be deducted to pay your share of federal and state income taxes before you get your take-home pay. **Take-home pay** is the amount of money in your paycheck after all deductions have been made. In addition to these deductions, **FICA taxes** will also be deducted before you receive your take-home pay. FICA taxes are deductions from your salary to cover Social Security and Medicare. These taxes are 4.2 percent for Social Security ($1323) and 1.45 percent for Medicare ($456.75) of your salary. (This figure is subject to change on a year-to-year basis.)

When you deduct your federal taxes of $8820, your state income taxes of $2205, and your total FICA taxes of $1779.75, your annual take-home pay is now $18,695.25, assuming you have no more deductions taken from your salary for such things as benefits through your company. Dividing this amount by 12 months, you have $1557 a month to budget. This exercise helps you understand why you can't afford a $50,000 car, for example, and why you should be very careful to avoid huge credit card debts. Because costs vary greatly from one part of the country to another, estimating expenses is difficult, but for purposes of this exercise, assume the following monthly expenses, most of which are fixed expenses and may be estimated on the low side for some locations:

- Housing: $400 (this most likely assumes you have a roommate)
- Transportation: $400 (includes car payment, gas, car insurance)
  - Car payment: $250 (this is most likely a small, inexpensive, compact car that is financed for 60 months)
  - Gas: $100 (if you have a long commute, this could be much more)
  - Car insurance: $50 (this varies widely from state to state and is much higher if the driver has had traffic violations or a DUI)
- Utilities (heat, electric, water): $80
- Student loans: $175

You have about $502 left for food, clothes, entertainment, telephone, cable TV, and so on. Right away it becomes apparent that having someone with whom to share expenses is an advantage. Complete the other items of this budget with amounts that you would allocate if this were your personal situation. Most of these items are variable expenses. How would you stretch $502 to cover these expenses?

- Food
- Medical expenses (not covered by insurance)
- Dental expenses (not covered by insurance)
- Car repairs and maintenance
- Internet/cable provider
- Home telephone
- Cell phone
- Entertainment
- Clothing
- Credit cards
- Education (if you are pursuing additional education or specialized training)
- Miscellaneous (shampoo, deodorant, magazines, etc.)
- Savings/investments
- Day care (if you have children)

This exercise can be painful, but is a valuable lesson to learn as early as possible. The good news is that you can increase your income and lessen the pressure on your budget, provided you realize that no matter how much money you make, it is easy to spend it unwisely on frivolous items that are soon forgotten.

Though you are urged to make wise financial decisions, you are encouraged to enjoy life and not be so thrifty that you don't allow yourself to spend money on things and items that bring you pleasure and enjoyment. If you learn early to budget, save, and make wise decisions about your expenditures, you should gain the ability to spend more freely on enjoyment and entertainment items as your salary increases.

Budgeting may seem overwhelming at first, and you may have trouble making ends meet until you learn to manage your money wisely. Here are a few tips that might help:

- Plan your meals carefully each week.
- Take a list to the grocery store and don't buy anything that is not on your list.
- Buy generic instead of brand-name items.
- Buy in bulk from large discount stores.
- Live at home with your parents while you pay your student loans, if you can.
- Live close to your work to save on transportation.
- Use public transportation if you can.
- Take your lunch instead of eating out.
- Eliminate a land line and use only your cell phone.
- Eliminate cable television or certain add-ons if they are too expensive for your budget.
- Avoid expensive drinks, such as lattes, that have no nutritional value.
- Get a part-time job until you have paid off your student loans and credit cards.

Now, access the Digital Briefcase on page 51 and complete the Personal Budget Planner.

WHAT YOU NEED TO KNOW ABOUT STUDENT LOANS

Why Didn't Someone Explain This to Me?

The high cost of college makes tuition out of reach for many families. For many students, if not most, the only way they can attend college is via student loans. If this is the only way you can go to college, borrow the money—but borrow no more than you absolutely must. Unlike other forms of financial aid, education loans must be repaid—with interest. Still, most students use loans to help pay for college. If you're unable to meet all your college costs through other means like scholarships, current family income, part-time jobs, and savings, then saying "yes" to a college loan is a smart move.

Borrowing Tips

Wise borrowers keep these tips about student loans in mind so that they graduate with as little debt as possible:

- Borrow only what you need to cover education expenses. You don't have to borrow the full amount offered in the financial aid award letter.
- Consider working while in school.
- Look for ways to keep living costs down, such having a roommate, using a budget, and packing your lunch.
- Try to finish your college education in the fastest time possible. Every semester means another student loan.

It's also a good idea to keep close track of your loan debt and, when possible, avoid borrowing from multiple programs and lenders (College Board, 2011).

GRADUATE *Quote*

Kerrie Dee
Graduate!
Bryant and Stratton College,
Orchard Park, New York
Career: Medical Assistant

My education made me marketable and employable. I now have skills that I could carry anywhere. My advice to you would be to work hard and don't take anything for granted. Get a support team at home and at school and get it quickly. I would also advise you to follow your heart and your passion. To work in a job you love, you must love what you do.

Repaying Student Loans

According to Torabi (2011), the median student loan debt is at record levels due to rising tuition costs and has now reached an average of $23,000; many students owe much more than this. If you are one of the many students who has borrowed money to go to college, you are probably concerned about your ability to repay the loans while maintaining a good quality of life after you graduate. Before you graduate or transfer, find out everything you need to know about your loan and determine your options. Some of the most pertinent points about student loans are as follows:

- You have a legal obligation to repay your student loans with interest.
- Bankruptcy will not eliminate your obligation to repay any student loans.
- You should get the addresses and phone numbers of lenders before you leave college. Certain circumstances, such as graduate school, allow you to defer your payments. A deferment allows you to postpone your payments, but you will still have to pay these loans with interest.
- Learn all the options you have for repaying your loans. Based on your salary, expenses, and budget, decide which one is best for you. Do this before you leave school!
- If for some reason you cannot make your payment, let the lender know immediately. This is not something that will go away. You do not want to default on your loan, as this will cause you to have a bad credit rating, prohibit you from holding a government job, and prohibit you from getting a tax refund while the loan is repaid.

Following are some do's and don'ts regarding student loans:

Do's

- Get the lender's policies in writing and read them carefully.
- Consolidate your loans if possible and go with the lender that offers you the most benefits, not just the ones required by law.
- Learn what kind of protection you have if you are late with a payment.
- Conduct an Internet search to determine if your FFELP lender is an authorized federal lender.
- Refer to the following website, which includes excellent questions and information to use when identifying a lender for your student loans: www.sfasu.edu/faid/programs/lenderlist.asp.

- If possible, consolidate your loans while you are in your grace period (six months after you graduate) because the interest rate will be lower.

- Complete your consolidation application and send it in before June 30 if possible, because interest rates are most likely to increase on July 1.

Don'ts

- Don't consolidate with anyone but a bona fide lender—not a marketing company.

- Do not use the U.S. Department of Education as a lender with which to consolidate your loans; they offer a very poor benefit package.

- Avoid consolidating with marketing companies, and be aware that many will use terms that sound like government terminology.

- Be careful about being hooked by a lender promising a cash rebate. The odds are favorable that a reduced rate will save you much more money than a rebate.

- Avoid companies that offer free gifts in order to get your consolidation package. This practice is prohibited by federal law. If a company is using this tactic, they are a marketing company and not a bona fide lender.

- If a lender does not state all the terms of benefits in writing, you should not sign up with them.

What Happens If You Default on Student Loans

As mentioned previously, you have a legal obligation to repay student loans, and nothing relieves you from that obligation. Still, people default and suffer the consequences. Some of the actions that can be taken to recover the loan include the following:

- Your federal income tax refund can be intercepted by the government until the debt is paid. The Department of Education collects millions of dollars in delinquent loans every year.

- Up to 15 percent of your paycheck can be garnished each month (meaning the lender can take this amount from your check).

- The government can take part of your Social Security benefits or disability benefits (though it cannot take an amount that would leave you with less than $750 per month).

- The government and private lenders can sue you to recover student loan debts. There are no time limitations on your being sued for delinquent student loan debts.

There are numerous websites that can provide additional information regarding defaulting on student loans and how to handle it if this happens to you. One site is www.nolo.com/legal-encyclopedia/default-student-loan-29859.html.

The best tip we can give you about student loans is this one: When you graduate, pay the loan off as quickly as you can. Consider the examples in Figure 2.1.

Read, Read, Read about Loans

As stated earlier, most students borrow money to attend college. It can also be said that most have no idea what they are getting themselves into, nor do they understand that it could take them 25 years or longer to repay the loan. This is one of the most serious decisions you will ever make, so read everything you can get your hands on about student loans and proceed with caution. Remember: you don't have to take everything that is offered you. Accept only the amount that you absolutely must have to cover your tuition, books, and other necessary expenses.

> To achieve the things you want, you need to understand your relationship with money, your belief system, and why you act the way you do.
> —Farnoosh Torabi

Figure 2.1   Total Interest Paid

Amount of Money Borrowed Paid by You	Your Interest Rate (Average)	Total Years to Repay (20 Years Is the Average)	Your Monthly Payment	Total Interest (Your Cost to Borrow the Money)
$5,000	7%	10	$58.05	$1,966.00
		20	$38.76	$4,302.40
		30	$33.27	$6,977.20
$10,000	7%	10	$116.11	$3,933.20
		20	$77.53	$8,607.20
		30	$66.53	$13,950.80
$15,000	7%	10	$174.16	$5,899.20
		20	$116.29	$12,909.60
		30	$99.80	$20,928.00
$20,000	7%	10	$232.22	$7,866.40
		20	$155.06	$17,214.40
		30	$133.06	$27,901.60
$30,000	7%	10	$348.33	$11,799.60
		20	$232.59	$25,821.60
		30	$199.59	$41,852.40

GOOD VERSUS BAD LOANS

How Do I Make Wise Decisions?

Credit card companies' dream customers are college students. In many cases, college students know very little about credit; they don't have a lot of cash so they frequently get themselves deep in debt. So beware of strangers bearing gifts in the form of credit card applications—they are the "fox in the hen house."

If you already have credit cards, you may want to access www.federalreserve.gov/creditcard and read more about the new government regulations related to credit cards. While credit card debt can still wreak havoc on your financial position, some of the new changes are a great improvement. The new laws include the following:

- Credit card companies cannot change fees, terms, or interest rates without a 45-day notice.
- Payments must come due on the same day every month.
- Credit card companies must provide information that details how long it will take you to pay a debt if you pay only the minimum. (Pay attention to this one!)

- The credit card company cannot change your interest rates during the first year you have the card. For example, if the rate is 13 percent when you open the account, it cannot change for a year unless it is an introductory rate (beware of these) or if you are more than 60 days late in paying your bill.

- Interest rate increases can only be applied to new charges; your old charges will still carry the same rate as before. (Adapted from Farnoosh Torabi's blog, New Credit Card Laws Take Effect, www.farnoosh.tv/financial-basics/debt-management/new-credit-card-laws-take-effect.)

Credit Card Assessment Exercise

Using the form in Figure 2.2 , list each of your credit cards, the interest percentage that you pay, the amount paid each month, the amount owed on each card, and a comment on how you feel about each card. For example, is this the one that you should pay off quickly because it has the lowest balance? Or should you pay another one off quickly because it has the highest interest rate? After you have completed this form, construct a plan for paying off your credit card debts. This means you will have to do something different from what you are doing now. Will you get a part-time job? Will you pack your lunch? Will you put your credit cards in a safe place and stop charging? Do you need to get a roommate or live at home for awhile?

An example is provided and some of the major credit card companies are listed. Add others that you may have.

Now that you have a picture of what you owe, make decisions about how you are going to get this debt off your back. Motivate yourself by thinking about how great it will feel to not

> *If you are making the minimum payments on $20,000 in credit card debt at 8%, it will take you 23.5 years to pay it off. At 19% (US average), it would take you 46 years.*
>
> *—Opportunity Debt Management*

have this debt hanging over your head. In the space below, describe your plan to pay off your credit card debt.

_____

_____

_____

_____

The ability to borrow money and to use credit can be very positive factors in your life if you learn to use it wisely. If you don't already have a credit card, you should get one credit card—no more than two. Actually, it is easier to get a credit card as a student than it is as an employee. Once you have a credit card, make a purchase of an amount that you are able to pay in full when it comes due. Do this several times, and you are beginning to establish a solid credit rating. One of the smartest ways you can establish good credit is to charge things on your credit card and pay off the entire amount every month, so that you never pay any interest.

If you fall into the credit card trap of making only the minimum payment and you continue to rack up large bills, you will soon find yourself in a deep hole that will be very hard to dig out. If you make a late payment, your credit card company will immediately raise your interest rate. Not only will that specific credit card company raise your interest rate, all the other companies with which you have credit cards might also raise your rates. All they need is a good excuse to start gouging you!

Credit card companies have implemented new strategies to charge you exorbitant rates. In some cases, the payment window has been shortened, making it much easier for you to be late with your payment. If you couldn't pay your bills when your interest rate was 14.9 percent, how are you going to pay it when they raise it to 29.9 percent or higher? Interest rate is the percent of interest you are charged each month on the total amount you owe the credit card company. This amount is added to the principal, which is the amount of money you charged or borrowed.

An even worse scenario is to charge the maximum on several credit cards and to begin making only the minimum payment.

If you continue making partial payments, the interest charges are calculated on the new credit card debt. So you end up paying interest on the last month's interest too. Thus your credit card debt accumulates rapidly and soon you find that what was once a relatively small amount of credit card debt has ballooned into a big amount which you find almost impossible to pay. Moreover, if you don't control your spending habits, your credit card debt rises even faster. This is how the vicious circle of credit card debt works. (Geyer, 2011)

> _Millions of Americans are attempting to pay off $450 billion to credit card companies._
> —Alexander Daskaloff, _Credit Card Debt_

Another pitfall that affects many people is the ploy used by credit card companies to allow you to skip a month without making a payment because "you are such a good customer." The credit card companies are taking care of themselves—not you. The interest keeps accumulating while you enjoy this so-called "free" month. You are simply getting deeper in debt, not saving.

While addressing pitfalls, you also need to be very much aware that transferring balances to those credit card companies that promise you a low rate of interest for several months or a year may not be the "gift" it appears to be. This is not the same as paying off a debt—it's just moving the misery around. In most cases, this practice simply prolongs the agony. If, for example, you owe money on that card already, the money you send to the credit card company will be applied to the part of the debt you already owe at the higher rate of interest; you could pay for a year and never reduce the debt you transferred if you are not paying attention to the fine print. Plus, you will pay a fee for transferring the money, which increases your debt. Remember: Credit card companies don't want you to know the real truth. Whatever they are offering you is a deal for them, not you!

The only way to get off the credit card merry-go-round is to stop charging, pay more than the minimum, and try to get the credit card company to lower your interest rate. Call the company, ask to speak to a supervisor, and insist on a lower rate. Sometimes this works.

Be wary of **credit counseling services.** These companies offer to help you get out of credit card debt by negotiating on your behalf with your creditors. While some are credible, many are not. If company representatives say the company is a non-profit, this simply means the business shows no profit at the end of the year, but they can still pay themselves big salaries and bonuses. If you contract a debt counseling service, this may show on your credit report and may call your credit worthiness into question. "It is wise to seek credit counseling through a service accredited by the Association of Independent Consumer Credit Counseling Agencies or the National Foundation for Credit Counseling. It is far less likely that an accredited organization will charge excessive fees or try to take advantage of you, than it is for an organization which is not accredited" (Larson, 2011). For more information, access www.expertlaw.com/library/finance/goodcreditcounselor.html.

A positive credit rating can help you make important large purchases; conversely, a poor credit rating can prohibit you from being able to buy a car or a house. Getting this credit card business straight is so important to your future. We highly recommend that you take time to read some of the references listed at the end of this chapter and take steps to reduce credit card debt immediately—starting today! Study Figure 2.2 carefully for more good tips on how to manage credit cards.

> *Anyone of the opinion money will do everything may well be suspected of doing everything for money.*
> —Benjamin Franklin

Auto Title Loans, Payday Loans, and Check Cashing Centers—Dangerous Credit Sources

Don't even think about an auto title loan, a payday loan, or a check cashing service! They are worse than credit card debt! This is highway robbery but is legal in most states. Some state legislatures have made these loans and services illegal, but in many states, you are fair game.

Figure 2.2 Check It Out

Before accepting a credit card, check the following items carefully:

- Look for the lowest permanent interest rate.

- Look for credit cards with low or no annual fees. If you will pay your credit card bill off every month, no annual fee is important. Remember that even the best card can be expensive if you don't pay the full amount due each month.

- Don't accept a credit card simply because you can get it or you are offered a high credit limit. Avoid having too many cards. The more cards you own, the more likely you are to get in credit card trouble.

- Read the terms of the credit card offer as well as the disclosure statement that comes with a card. Check for annual fees, late payment fees, over-the-limit fees, account set-up fees, cash advance fees, and the method used to calculate balances.

- Be careful of low introductory rates. These special rates can last for short periods of time and then skyrocket once the introductory period is over if you are late with a payment.

- Call the issuer and make sure they report to a credit agency—you want any positive payment history that you build to be reflected in your credit report.

Comparative credit card rates can be found on the New York State Banking Department's website and are available to consumers for free at www.cardratings.com/surveyhome.html.

Source: Adapted from State of New York Banking Department, 2011.

> The Consumer Federation of America (CFA) is warning consumers to exercise extreme caution when using Internet payday loan sites, where loans due by the next payday can cost up to $30 per $100 borrowed and borrowers typically face annual interest rates (APRs) of 650%.
>
> —Robert Longley

First, let's look at automobile title loans. What happens in the case of an automobile title loan is that you literally use your car title to secure a high-interest loan, usually no longer than 30 days. This means that if you as the borrower cannot repay the loan within 30 days, the lender can take your car and sell it to get the loan money back. Many title lenders will not make the loan if you owe anything on your car.

Auto title lenders often target people with bad credit, low-income individuals, military members, and elderly people—in other words, people who are vulnerable and may be desperate to borrow money. These lenders make money from high-interest loans and by selling cars they have repossessed from customers who cannot repay their loans. If you are desperate for cash, an auto loan may seem like a good idea, but this is a short-term solution and the effects can be devastating (South Carolina Appleseed Legal Justice Center, 2010).

If the borrower can't pay the loan on the due date, many lenders will roll it over, which compounds the problem because the high rate of interest continues to build. The paperwork may show that you borrowed the money at 25 percent (which is exorbitant), but this rate over a year is actually 300 percent. This is worse than highway robbery! Unless you are willing to pay the highest kind of interest rates and risk losing your car, you should avoid these loans at all costs.

Payday loans are simply more bad news. These loans are extremely expensive cash advances that must be repaid in full on the borrower's next payday to keep the personal check required to secure the loan from bouncing. The average payday loans cost 470 percent annual interest. Cash-strapped consumers run the risk of becoming trapped in repeat borrowing due to triple-digit interest rates, unaffordable repayment terms, and coercive collection tactics made possible by check holding. In one state almost 60 percent of the loans made are either same-day renewals or new loans taken out immediately after paying off the prior loan.

Tips for Managing Your Credit

- Don't borrow or spend more than you can afford.
- Pay the full balance on your credit card bill each month. If you can't, at least pay more than the minimum amount due.
- Pay bills as soon as they arrive. In addition to incurring late-payment charges, a late payment can result in higher rates on all your other accounts. Creditors can check your credit report regularly, and seeing a late payment may give them reason to raise interest rates.
- Call and have the due date changed if a payment falls at a time of the month when you may be short on cash.
- Opt out of special services that credit card lenders offer, such as fraud protection, insurance, travel club, as so on. Turn down free trial offers that will be billed automatically to your credit card if you forget to cancel.
- Once a year, order your credit report. Check it for accuracy. If any information is inaccurate, dispute it immediately.
- Build a payment history beyond your credit history by using the services of PRBC. Once you enroll, PRBC will keep a payment history of your rental, utility, and other recurring bill payments and provide that information to the three credit reporting bureaus. To learn more, visit www.payrentbuildcredit.com (State of New York Banking Department, 2011).

Payday lenders use coercive tactics to collect their money in many cases. They might threaten you with negative credit ratings on specialized databases and credit reports. Consumers can lose their bank accounts if they have a record of bouncing checks used to get payday loans. Some lenders will threaten criminal charges or court martial if military personnel fail to cover their loans (PayDay Loan Consumer Information, 2010).

Internet payday lending businesses are just as bad as payday lenders, if not worse. By borrowing money on the Internet, you run the risk of security and fraud. In some cases, loans are directly deposited into the borrower's bank account and electronically withdrawn the next payday. Many of these loans are structured to automatically renew every payday, with the exorbitant finance charge electronically withdrawn from the borrower's bank account. Be aware that these loans are often offered with a clever rebate scheme to circumvent states' laws regarding this type of loan (PayDay Loan Consumer Information, 2010).

Check cashing services should be avoided like the plague because they charge astronomical fees. They charge you a high fee to "hold a check" until payday comes around. We know that sometimes your money may not last until the end of the week or month, but getting involved in this vicious cycle only means losing more of your hard-earned, much-needed money. In a recent phone call to several payday loan and check cashing centers, the fee to "hold" a check for $100 for one week averaged $16.50. Therefore, after one week, the amount owed would be $116.50.

That doesn't sound too bad, but if something happened and you had to have them "hold" the check for a while (that is to say, if you had to wait a month or two to pay them back) then this really becomes "a loan" and the $16.50 actually represents an annual percentage rate (APR) of 430 percent. That figure is not a typo: four hundred and thirty percent! The highest APR for even the most expensive credit cards averages only 21 to 30 percent. Again, we use the word *astronomical.*

If you need extra cash until payday, make every effort to borrow it from a friend or family member. In the long run, this will cost you much less. Payday loans, auto title loans, and check cashing services are highly controversial companies that continue to face many legal battles as well as negative perception by the public. The reason they operate is a simple fact: they are highly lucrative businesses that make money by preying on people who are desperate and can't get money anywhere else. If at all possible, avoid these services at all costs!

> 41% of workers often live paycheck to paycheck. More than half said they would need $500 more per paycheck to live comfortably.
>
> —CareerBuilder.com

THE ALL-IMPORTANT FICO SCORE

Do You Know What Affects Your Credit Score?

You need to know the score—the FICO score! FICO stands for Fair Isaac Corporation. Financial guru Suze Orman (2007) says, "Just about every financial move you will make for the rest of your life will be somehow linked to your FICO score. Not knowing how your score is calculated, how it is used, and how you can improve it will keep you broke long past your young-and-fabulous days. The way the business world sees it, your FICO score is a great tool to size up how good you will be at handling a new loan or a credit card, or whether you're a solid citizen to rent an apartment to." If you have a high FICO score, you will get better interest rates. Your FICO score can affect everything from your ability to finance a house to being able to get reasonable automobile insurance premiums.

So what is this thing called a FICO score? This carefully researched information based on your credit history, income, and ability to repay your debts is a score that determines your level of future credit risk. Your FICO score is a three-digit number based on your borrowing and bill-paying history and is an important component of your overall financial profile. In general, a credit score can range from a low of 300 to a high of 850. Most scores fall in the 600 or 700 range (Consumers Union, 2007). "Generally speaking, a score of 750 or higher is considered in the top tier. Anything below 650 is at the other end of the spectrum" (Slade, 2011). "How important is all of this? The Consumer Federation of America estimates that someone with a bad credit score would be charged more than $5000 than someone with a good score on a five-year $20,000 car loan" (Slade, 2011).

You may also hear this score referred to as your **credit report**. Your credit report is a detailed collection of your entire credit history.

There are three major credit scoring companies in the United States: TransUnion, Equifax, and Experian. The following information explains how you can get your FICO score.

When You Can Obtain a Free Copy of Your Credit Report

- Once every year
- If you have been denied credit in the previous 60 days
- If you have been denied employment or insurance in the previous 60 days
- If you suspect someone has been fraudulently using your accounts or your identity
- If you are unemployed and plan on applying for employment within the next 60 days
- If you are on public assistance
- When applying for a mortgage

Request your free annual credit report from each of the three major agencies every year and check it carefully for suspicious activity. Order all three reports online at www.annualcredit report.com or by calling 1-877-322-8228. You will go through a simple verification process, and your reports will be mailed to you (State of New York Banking Department, 2011).

Your credit score will be based on several criteria, including how much debt you have, how many credit cards you have, how many of your credit cards carry balances, how long you have had outstanding debt, your debt-to-income ratio, how many late payments you have made, how much credit you have available, and your overall history of paying your debts on time. One of the most important factors in your credit score is how much available credit you have (Consumers Union, 2007).

FICO scores are checked when you try to purchase a car or a house, and increasingly for a variety of other reasons. It is common now for potential employers to check credit scores before extending a job offer, so it is important to know what your credit score is and to take steps to build an acceptable score. If your credit score falls in the low 600s, you might be considered for a loan with a higher rate of interest, sometimes known as a subprime loan, if you are considered at all. You will be required to pay a higher rate of interest, assuming your loan is approved, because you would be considered a high risk. Consider the information in Figure 2.3.

If you are turned down for a loan, you are entitled to get a free copy of your credit report, provided you ask for it within six months of being rejected (State of New York Banking Department, 2007).

If you have already done things that cause you to have a low credit score, you can rectify that by beginning to change your habits now. We highly recommend that you request a copy of your credit report to determine your FICO score, to see if you may have a problem, and to determine

Figure 2.3 The Impact of FICO on Buying a Home

FICO Score	Interest Rate	Payment	30 Years of Interest
500	9.3%	$1651	$394,362
560	8.5%	$1542	$355,200
620	7.3%	$1373	$294,247
675	6.1%	$1220	$239,250
700	5.6%	$1151	$214,518

what the concerns are. In fact, we recommend that you get a credit report from each of the three of the major credit bureaus. Different companies report to different agencies, and you need to get the entire big picture. If you find that a mistake has been made on your credit report, you should notify the credit bureau and dispute the information. The credit bureau is required to investigate. A helpful place to begin is to check out the tutorials at www.bankrate.com under "Debt Management."

Getting the best FICO score possible is very important to your bottom line and can be the difference in paying $100 more a month on your car payment or getting a 6 percent mortgage rather than 7.5 percent. You can obtain a credit report from one or all three companies. The addresses and contact information for all three major companies are located below (Consumers Union, 2007). Use this information to complete the following exercise.

Equifax	**Experian**	**Transunion**
P.O. Box 740241	P.O. Box 2002	P.O. Box 1000
Atlanta, GA 30374-0241	Allen, TX 75013	Chester, PA 19022
800-685-111	888-322-5583	800-888-4213
www.equifax.com	www.experian.com	www.transunion.com

Go online to one or all of the companies listed above and request a credit report. If you find erroneous information that could damage your credit, call the reporting company to see what you can do about it. You can receive one free credit report per year by logging onto www.freecreditreport.com.

Summarize the findings of your credit report:

_____

_____

_____

_____

_____

After obtaining a copy of your credit report, determine how you can improve your FICO score or keep your FICO score high.

_____

_____

_____

_____

_____

Keeping Your FICO Score Healthy

According to Orman (2007), there are several key ways to improve your FICO score:

- Pay your bills on time. (This shows you are responsible.)
- Manage your debt-to-credit-limit ratio. (This is the sum of what you owe compared to what banks think you can afford to borrow.)

Everett Collection/Alamy

How can financial television programs and books, such as those by Suze Orman, improve your financial I.Q.?

- Protect your credit history. (Rather than canceling credit cards that you have a good history of paying, just destroy the cards and stop using them; you have not destroyed the history.)
- Create the right credit mix. (Lenders want to see a reasonable mix of credit cards, retail cards, and installment loans. This does not mean that you should accept every credit card that is offered to you!)

MAKING WISE FINANCIAL DECISIONS BEYOND COLLEGE YEARS

How Do I Stay on Track to Build Financial Stability?

After you graduate from college, many of your financial decisions will change. Instead of trying to figure out how to pay for books and tuition, you will most likely be focused on buying a car, purchasing a house, saving for retirement, supporting a family, and making wise investment decisions. In order to make good decisions, you need to fully understand your paycheck and the tax system.

Plan Today for Tomorrow's Retirement

While preparing to graduate from college and immediately after you graduate, you will be faced with many decisions. If you have not done so already, you will have to make decisions about which job to accept, what area to live in, what kind of home you can afford, whether you should keep a car you own now or purchase a new one, whether to get married now or in the near future, whether to have a roommate or to live alone—the list goes on and on.

Most college graduates deal with this list of decisions, and most make reasonable decisions. This list, however, does not include one of the most important priorities: financial management. Most people fail to give the same kind of attention to financial matters that they do to other major areas of their lives. The average person spends more time deciding which programs to watch on TV than on which financial choices to make. Young college graduates often assume that they do not have enough money to manage, and these decisions will be important only when they are much older. Nothing could be further from the truth! The first day you go to work is the day you should start planning for retirement and financial security!

Before you accept a job, find out what options you have for retirement. Does the company offer a guaranteed pension (not many companies do anymore)? Do they offer a 401(k)? Do they offer any matching funds based on the amount you are saving yourself? Planning for retirement is one of your most important decisions. Start immediately when you get that first permanent job! This decision is much too important to ignore or put off until later! If you don't understand the program, get an appointment with a human relations manager in the company and ask questions. You can work hard all your life and end up with nothing unless you are smart now!

BIGGEST INTERVIEW *Blunders*

John interviewed with ACE Design Company and accepted the job without asking anything about the retirement plan. Later he learned that ACE offered neither a guaranteed retirement plan nor a 401(k). The Design It Right Company, on the other hand, offered a guaranteed pension and a 401(k). Too late, John realized that he turned down a better job even though the salary was higher at the job he accepted. What can you learn from John's mistakes?

LESSON: When considering two or more job offers, give consideration to the benefits package, which may save you a great deal of out-of-pocket cash.

> *Money does grow on trees—the trees of patience.*
>
> *—Proverb*

Understand Your Paycheck

Many new college graduates are not prepared for the amount of taxes that are deducted from their paychecks. Unless you have worked and paid taxes, you may be in for a big surprise. You will have deductions made for federal and state taxes, FICA (Social Security taxes), as well as other deductions for benefits to which you must contribute.

When you begin a new job, you will be asked to complete paperwork that details the number of dependents, or the number of individuals you are supporting, that you want to claim. If you have only yourself, you might want to claim none. This will help ensure that enough taxes are deducted from your paycheck so that you don't owe money on April 15; instead, you might be fortunate enough to get a refund. The more dependents you claim, the more money flows to you with each paycheck.

You may complete your own tax return or you may seek the services of a qualified tax preparation service to assist you in preparing your tax return. Regardless, you should set up a file at the beginning of each fiscal year and keep your documentation for expenses. If you don't know anything about filing a tax return, you need to talk to someone who can provide detailed advice.

You will need to hold onto your W-2 form, which declares how much your income and taxes

> *Did you ever notice that when you put the words "The" and "IRS" together, it spells "THEIRS"?*
>
> *—Unknown*

for the year were. Your employer will send the W-2 to you or distribute it at work. You should have file folders for medical bills, insurance, taxes (cars and house), home office (if you are eligible to declare one), and any other areas that you might need for completing your tax return. Keep records of taxes that you paid on your house or cars. If you purchased a house during this year, certain parts of those expenses are deductible. Of course, children are deductible as dependents, as is child care. Most charitable gifts to churches, the Red Cross, United Way, and many other charities are deductible.

If you keep your papers filed and organized all year, it will take you much less time to get your tax information together and you are much less likely to overlook something you could deduct or need to report. Take advantage of every write-off you can by keeping good records.

Buying Your First Car

Most people love a new car, and many love fancy, expensive cars. Regardless of how much you like them, cars are not one of the best places to spend your money. Unless you live in a big city with good transportation services, however, a car is a necessity for getting back and forth to work and for recreational purposes. Buying a car can be a very confusing and frustrating experience for anyone, especially someone who knows very little about the lingo and sales techniques used by many auto salespeople. One of the first things to do is to make up your mind that you aren't going to fall in love with a car and buy it until you have done extensive homework. If you know very little about buying a car, comparing one brand to another, finance charges, and the like, take someone with you who does.

Smart money tip: Never buy a new car! Buying a new car is a very poor use of your money. As soon as you drive the new car off the dealership lot, the value plummets.

Can you really afford this car and have money left for essential expenses?

Shutterstock

Rather than buy a new car, search for a very good used car that is one to three years old. You can usually purchase an extended warranty on a pre-owned car. You will get a car that most likely looks like the current model, you will save lots of money, and most people will not know if it is new or used. Not only will the price be lower, but so will the taxes and insurance.

Here are some major points that you should consider when buying a car:

- Do your homework! This is too important a decision to take lightly. Research, research, research! Go to a website like Consumer Guide (http://consumerguideauto.howstuff works.com) to search for prices or J. D. Power to check on consumer satisfaction.

- Know how much you can afford each month before you even start looking. Should you buy or lease? A deal that allows you to buy a new car for $160 a month may sound good, but what is the residual fee at the end? What happens if you go over the allowed 12,000 miles? Can you live within a prescribed number of miles? If you lease, you will typically have a lower down payment and a lower monthly payment, and you can drive a newer car every two to three years. But you don't own the car, you don't accumulate equity, and you have a limited number of miles you can drive. Leasing is usually more expensive in the long run. Wear and tear on the car can change the residual value (what the car is worth at the end of your lease) and cost you more money when it is time to turn the car in to the dealership.

> *The more confused you are, the better chance the auto salesperson has at making a fat profit off of you. Auto dealers are kings of creating confusion.*
> —Suze Orman, author and TV host

- Use a payment calculator to help you determine the real costs.

- Take the car for a test drive: Does it have blind spots? Is it noisy?

- Depending on your family needs and your budget, should you buy a sport utility vehicle, a sedan, a subcompact, a compact?

- What is the EPA rating? This is a good indicator of how much gas your car will use.

- How much are the insurance and taxes? If you buy a "hot" car, your insurance premiums will cost you more! If you have traffic violations, your insurance will be higher.

- For what kind of interest rate do you qualify?

- Should you consider a hybrid?

- How well does each model retain its value?

- What kind of service charges can you expect? Some are very high, so find out!

- If you are buying a used car, have it carefully inspected by your mechanic.

- Set your price before you start looking. Don't forget the added fees of title, tag, and so forth.

- Negotiate! Don't ever take the first price offered to you.

- Wait 24 hours before you sign anything!

- Look at all the financing options. They are not all created equal. Credit union financing is often better than many others. Dealer financing is often higher.

- Above all—be prepared to walk away if you don't get the deal you need and want. If anything appears fishy or if the salesman seems shifty, keep looking. (Ciminillo, 2010)

Based on the points discussed above, describe the car that you think you should consider buying. Research information about this car and compare it to others in its class. Include price, costs of insurance and taxes, description, model, and year and justify your decision.

_____

_____

_____

_____

PUTTING IT ALL TOGETHER

Some of the points mentioned throughout this book will have a major impact on your life and your lifestyle, but none will be more important than making wise financial management decisions. These decisions include daily budgeting, credit card choices, retirement options, savings programs, and benefit packages. Making the right financial decisions requires taking time to educate yourself about the options. You cannot afford not to prepare yourself to make wise financial decisions!

DIGITAL BRIEFCASE

ESTIMATING INCOME AND EXPENSES

Now that you have become familiar with the terms and the process of budgeting, assume you have a new job and that you want to begin living on a budget right away. A comprehensive budget planning exercise follows that will help you learn to manage your money carefully.

For purposes of this exercise, you will estimate all your income and expenses. Later, you can plug in the actual amount and determine the difference in what you estimated and the actual amount. All sections of the Personal Budget Planner will not be applicable to you at this point, but they will as your income grows and your personal situation changes.

Use the following steps to identify and estimate your sources of income. For purposes of this exercise, we are going to assume that your beginning salary is $35,000 and that you have no other income. (It should be interesting to you to determine beginning salaries in your major as a part of this budgeting experience.)

- Assume that you are earning $35,000 annually with your first job. This is known as gross salary and is the amount of money you make before taxes and other items are deducted.
- For purposes of this exercise, assume you are contributing 5 percent of your gross income to a tax-sheltered individual retirement account, although you might contribute up to 10 percent. An individual retirement account, often called an IRA, is a self-directed, tax-deferred retirement investment account established by employed workers who earn a salary, wage, or self-employment income. Using the amount of $35,000 as your gross salary, take 5 percent of this number and subtract it from the gross amount of your salary. Taxes will be based on this amount. You would figure your IRA contribution amount like this:

     $35,000.00
     $\times \quad .05$
     $1,750.00 (amount contributed to IRA)

- Now, subtract the amount contributed to an IRA and you will have your gross salary after the tax-sheltered amount has been deducted. This is the amount on which you will figure taxes.

     $35,000
     $- 1,750$
     $33,250 (gross salary after IRA has been deducted)

■ Now, estimate your net salary. Net salary is the amount you have left after taxes. Assume you are in the 28 percent tax bracket, that your state income taxes are 8 percent of your income, and that your FICA taxes (Medicare and Social Security) are 5.65 percent.

■ Using the $35,000 salary in the example above and considering that you have already subtracted the tax-sheltered amount, you would multiply .28 times $33,250 to determine your federal taxes.

$$\frac{\begin{array}{r} \$33,250.00 \\ \times \qquad .28 \end{array}}{\$9,310.00 \text{ (federal taxes)}}$$

■ Enter this amount in Section Two of the Personal Budget Planner under Federal Income Tax, Estimated Amount.

■ Then you would multiply 8 percent (.08) times $33,250 to get your state taxes and enter this number under State Income Tax, Estimated Amount, in Section Two of your Personal Budget Planner.

$$\frac{\begin{array}{r} \$33,250.00 \\ \times \qquad .08 \end{array}}{\$2,660.00 \text{ (state taxes)}}$$

■ Finally, you would multiply 5.65 percent (.0565) times $33,250 to determine your Social Security and Medicare taxes and enter this number in the Social Security/Medicare Tax column in Section Two of your Personal Budget Planner.

$$\frac{\begin{array}{r} \$33,250.00 \\ \times \qquad .0565 \end{array}}{\$1,878.00}$$

■ Now that you have figured all your taxes, add them together and subtract from $33,250 to get the net take-home pay for this example.

$$\frac{\begin{array}{r} \$9,310 \\ 2,660 \\ + \ 1,878 \end{array}}{\$13,848 \text{ (total taxes)}}$$

■ Now, subtract your total tax deductions in Section Two from your total estimated income in Section One, and you arrive at your spendable income.

$$\frac{\begin{array}{r} \$33,250 \text{ (gross salary after IRA deduction)} \\ - \ 13,848 \text{ (total taxes to be deducted)} \end{array}}{\$19,402 \text{ (net take home pay after taxes, or spendable income)}}$$

Spendable income is the amount you can actually budget.

■ This is the amount after all taxes and deductions have been made. For the $35,000 salary in this example, the net take home pay would be $19,402. Enter $19,402 under estimated amount for Net Salary in Section One of your Personal Budget Planner.

■ It is much easier to manage a budget if you set it up on a month-to-month basis. Now that you have determined your income after taxes and deductions, you can divide this amount by 12 to get the amount you can actually budget.

$19,402 \div 12 = $1,616 (This is your monthly spendable income and the amount you must divide among your expenses.)

PERSONAL BUDGET PLANNER

Using the information you learned in the previous paragraphs about figuring taxes, Social Security, and other items, complete the Personal Budget Planner below:

Personal Budget Planner
Section One: Income and Income Taxes Section—Annual

INCOME	ESTIMATED AMOUNT	ACTUAL AMOUNT	DIFFERENCE
Net Salary and Bonuses (after tax income)			
Interest Income			
Part-Time Jobs Income			
Investment Income			
Miscellaneous Income (gifts, etc.)			
Total Income			

Personal Budget Planner
Section Two: Income Tax Withheld

INCOME	ESTIMATED AMOUNT	ACTUAL AMOUNT	DIFFERENCE
Federal Income Tax			
State Income Tax			
Local Income Tax (may not be applicable)			
Social Security/Medicare Tax			
Income Taxes Subtotal			
Spendable Annual Income			

In the case of the previous example, this person would have $1616 per month. Right away you can see that this person most likely needs a roommate to share expenses and that he or she will have to budget carefully to cover expenses until they earn more money.

Now proceed to Section Three of the Personal Budget Planner and estimate your expenses for each category that is applicable. This section of the Personal Budget Planner allows you to track how you are spending your money.

Certain expenses will be paid biannually or annually. Convert these expenses to monthly amounts for budgeting purposes so you can be saving toward the date when they will come due. If they are annual payments, divide by 12 to determine the monthly amount. For example, if your car insurance is $658 for one year, your monthly cost is $658 ÷ 12 or $54.83 per month.

When you have completed this exercise, you will have a comprehensive picture of your annual and monthly income and expenses, and you will be able to determine if you have a surplus or a shortage and can make decisions accordingly. You were provided assistance for the first two sections of your Personal Budget Planner. Using the amounts provided as monthly take-home pay, you should now plan a budget using Section Three.

Now that you have completed this exercise, you should have a much better idea of how to manage your money on a monthly and annual basis.

Personal Budget Planner
Section Three: Estimated Annual/Monthly Expenses

CATEGORY	ANNUAL	MONTHLY (Divide by 12)	COMMENTS
Savings			
Investments			
Retirement (your IRA investment goes here)			
Housing			
Homeowner's/Renter's Insurance			
Property Taxes			
Home Repairs/Improvements			
Food (includes groceries, lunches, snacks, eating out)			
Transportation (includes car payments, gas/oil, etc.)			
Automobile Insurance			
Automotive Maintenance Fees, Repairs, Tolls			
Public Transportation			
Telephone—Cell			
Utilities (electricity, gas, water, sewer)			
Internet/Cable			
Student Loans			
Other Loans			
Credit Cards			
Medical Expenses			
Dental Expenses			
Fitness (gym, yoga, massage)			
Entertainment			
Vacations			
Pets (food, veterinarian, grooming)			
Day Care			
Education			
Clothing			
Insurance			
Miscellaneous (toiletries, household products, grooming, hair, makeup)			
Total Expenses			
Surplus/Shortage (your spendable income minus your expenses equals your surplus or shortage)			

REFERENCES

Ciminillo, J. (2010). Ten tips for buying a car. Retrieved April 2007 from www.howtojoinacu .org/services.tentips.cfm.

College Board. (2011). Student loan comparison calculator: Private/alternative loans. Retrieved March 15, 2011, from http://apps.collegeboard.com/loancompare /loancomparisonintro.jsp.

Consumers Union Organization. (2007). What is a credit score? Retrieved April 17, 2007, from www.consumersunion.org/creditmatters/creditmattersfactsheets/001633.html.

Daskaloff, A. (1999). *Credit card debt: Reduce your financial burdens in three easy steps.* New York: Avon Books.

Federal Reserve Bank of Boston. (2011). *Identity theft.* Retrieved from www.bostonfed.org /consumer/identity/idtheft.pdf.

Fowles, D. (2011). Five smart money moves for new college graduates. Retrieved April 14, 2007, from http://financialplan.about.com/od/college/a/SmartMoves.htm.

Geyer, J. (2011). What is credit card debt? Retrieved March 15, 2011, from http://hubpages .com/hub/What-is-Credt-Card-Debt.

Greentree Gazette, Federal Student Loan Consolidation Program. May 2009.

IRA Online Resource Guide. (2007). Information about Roth IRAs. Retrieved April 14, 2007, from www.irs.gov/retirement/article/0..id=137307.00.html.

Larson, A. (2011). Finding a good credit counseling service. Retrieved April 10, 2011, from www.expertlaw.com/library/finance/goodcreditcounselor.html.

Orman, S. (2007). *The money book for the young, fabulous, and broke.* New York: Riverhead Books.

PayDay Loan Consumer Information. (2010). Retrieved August 5, 2007, from www .paydayloaninfo.org/facts.cfm.

South Carolina Appleseed Legal Justice Center. (2004). Auto title loans and the law.

Slade, D. (March 13, 2011). Don't gamble with your credit score. *The State.*

State of New York Banking Department. (2011). Using credit wisely: What you need to know. Retrieved March 16, 2011, from www.banking.state.ny.us/brcw.htm.

Stephen F. Austin State University. FFELP loan program lender information. Retrieved April 9, 2011, from www.sfasu.edu/faid/programs/lenderlist.asp.

Torabi, F. (2011). Presentation at Pearson's Conference. Savannah, Georgia.

Taxable Income Brackets and Rates

What is the income range of your expected tax bracket shortly after graduation?

What is the rate (%) at which your income will be taxed?

What is FICA?

Some debts are fun when you are acquiring them, but none are fun when you set about retiring them.

- Ogden Nash

UNIVERSITY OF
SOUTH CAROLINA
College of Hospitality, Retail
and Sport Management

Annual Salary

Courtesy of Steinar/Shutterstock.

Annual Gross Pay = $_____

Annual net "take home" pay

after taxes = $_____

How much is this every two weeks? $_____

How much is this every month? $_____

What are some important reasons why we should choose to live by a monthly budget?

1.

2.

3.

4. Managed money goes _____!

> The successful leader must plan his work and work his plan.
>
> -Napoleon Hill

UNIVERSITY OF
SOUTH CAROLINA
College of Hospitality, Retail
and Sport Management

Saving, Building Wealth

Define "Roth IRA"

Define "Mutual Fund"

Define "Compound Interest"

Define "Discretionary income"

Name (Printed)_____

Signature _____

UNIVERSITY OF
SOUTH CAROLINA
College of Hospitality, Retail
and Sport Management

59

Salary Negotiation

Partner Activity

What is your expected starting salary range in your first position after college graduation?

Discuss and list three reasons why you are worth this salary.

1)

2)

3)

What you get by achieving your goals is not as important as what you become by achieving your goals

—Zig Ziglar

UNIVERSITY OF
SOUTH CAROLINA
College of Hospitality, Retail
and Sport Management

PART TWO:
MANAGING YOUR LIFE

chapter three

BUILD

BUILDING YOUR PROFESSIONAL IMAGE

Ethics is knowing the difference between what you have a right to do and what is right to do.
—Potter Stewart

PART TWO: MANAGING YOUR LIFE

Think about a belief that you hold dear. What is that belief? _____

_____

_____

_____

_____

How can this belief help guide you in your career or job-making decisions? _____

_____

_____

_____

_____

CREATING YOUR OWN PERSONAL BRAND—ME, INC.

Who Do You Want to Become?

Brands are everywhere. The Nike swoosh, the Starbucks cup, Levi rivets, the AT&T globe—the list goes on and on. Big companies understand the importance of establishing a distinctive brand. You need to take a lesson from big companies and establish a brand for yourself. You are literally the CEO of your own company: Me, Inc. As you prepare to interview for a job, you need to be preparing to market yourself. You should be striving to "develop the micro equivalent of the Nike Swoosh" (Peters, 1997). You need to develop your brand!

You have an opportunity to stand out and to develop your own brand, to become exactly what you want to be. You have to figure out how to create a distinctive role for yourself, a message that conveys who you are. As you work through this book, you may want to change parts of your brand, but the main thing for you to focus on right now is getting started.

> The remarkable thing we have is a choice every day regarding the attitude we will embrace for that day. We cannot change our past . . . We cannot change the fact that people will act in a certain way. We cannot change the inevitable. The only thing we can do is play on the one string we have, and that is our attitude.
>
> —Charles R. Swindoll

THE POWER OF OPTIMISM AND THE RIGHT ATTITUDE

What Do You Need to Improve?

You've heard it all your life: "You have a great attitude." Or maybe "You have a bad attitude." Or "You need to improve your attitude." Perhaps you have heard it said this way: "Attitude is not important—attitude is everything." Parents, teachers, coaches, and bosses all talk constantly about attitude. Why are attitude and optimism so important? Perhaps it is because what you think and how you feel about yourself has so much to do with how your perform at school and later at work. Attitude is important in all aspects of your life: school, work, relationships. A recent national survey asked the question, "What counts more: Employee aptitude; hard skills and technical competencies; employee attitude; or relational skills, motivation and positive outlook? Nearly 60% of corporations said attitude was the no. 1 concern" (Teamwork Newsletter, 2008).

Exactly what is attitude? Attitude is the manner in which you act or your views toward whatever is happening. For example, you may care about your schoolwork, or you may not be interested. You might treat people with respect, or you may be disrespectful toward some people. You either come to school on time and listen, or you get there late and slouch in your desk and look disgusted. You have a willing attitude at work or you have a "let somebody else do it" disposition. All of this has to do with your personal attitude.

Your attitude affects your performance at school and at work; it also affects others' performance because one person with a bad attitude can have a negative effect on everyone around him

Figure 3.1 Working on Yourself

- **Smile** even when you really just want to sit down and cry or when being grouchy and hurtful is easier than being nice. Greet everyone with a smile and good thoughts and feelings.

- **Push yourself** to be outgoing and friendly even when you feel shy and want to withdraw. Remember that most people feel shy and insecure at times. By being friendly, you will be helping others who are struggling.

- **Try to avoid worrying** about things that *might* happen. Deal with the here and now—that will usually be more than enough to keep you busy. It has been said that only 8 percent of our worries actually come true and they are usually small worries when they happen. Instead of worrying, focus your energy on doing great work at school or on your job.

- **Give people sincere compliments.** Tell them how nice they look or specifically what a great job they did. Look right at the person and brag on him or her. Being nice to someone else takes nothing away from you, and it wins friends and influences people if you are sincere.

- **Avoid getting caught up in the gossip mill.** Volunteer nice remarks about people when they are not present, especially if someone else is running them down. Stand up for people who are being mistreated when you can.

- **Try to be helpful to others**, especially someone who is having a really bad day or a difficult time in their

> Only 8 percent of our worries are actually over legitimate troubles. 40 percent of our worries never happen. 30 percent of our worries concern the past. 12 percent are needless worries about health. 10 percent are insignificant.
>
> —Dr. Walter Cavert

lives. Offer to pick up something for them or buy them lunch or just listen. Kindness is never forgotten, and everyone needs it.

- **Get up early and exercise for a few minutes** to get your adrenaline working. Meditate and concentrate on all the good things in your life. Count your blessings instead of your problems.

- **Rid yourself of negative baggage** that you have been carrying around with you—bad things that happened, and you keep bringing them up in your mind. Forgive yourself and others for things that happened in the past that hurt you. It is very important for you to forgive yourself! In your mind, put all the negative things you are still holding onto in a big suitcase. Take this suitcase into the forest and leave it there with all the negativity that you have been carrying around way too long. Now, pretend that you are walking out of the forest into the sunshine.

- **Be aware that everyone you meet is carrying some kind of burden or dealing with a problem.** A negative reaction from someone may be a reflection of a difficult problem they are struggling with rather than the fact they are simply not nice people. Try to listen to people's words but also their body language. Look at people around you. What can you do to help them? You will find that if you help others, you will feel better about yourself, and they will help you when you need it.

or her. Not only must you work on your personal attitude, you also have to learn not to let others make you feel bad about yourself or to put a damper on your day. So how do you get this magical attitude that makes things so much better for you and everyone with whom you come in contact? Consider the tips in Figure 3.1.

GETTING RID OF NEGATIVISM AND AVOIDING NEGATIVE PEOPLE

Who Drags You Down and Makes You Feel Small?

Do you allow people with negative attitudes to rub off on you?

Shutterstock

One thing you need to know is that you can't change anyone unless he or she wants to change—that includes people with negative attitudes. You can only change yourself and how you allow other people's negative attitudes to affect you. As you deal with certain people who make you feel small or put you down, consider your feelings after you have interacted with them. What was the result of your being in contact with that person? Did you feel worse or distressed or depressed? Did talking to a certain person make you begin to doubt your ability to do something that you really wanted to do? This is what attitude is all about—you simply can't let those people control you and your emotions. So what do you do to rid yourself of this negativism and negative people's attitudes? Study the tips in Figure 3.2.

Figure 3.2   Working on Relationships

- Make up your mind that you are in control of yourself and that you will not let anyone else steal your joy and optimism. This may take time. The person who makes you feel bad could be your mother or your significant other or a good friend. Is there a person or people who make you feel bad almost every time you interact with them? Sometimes you simply have to distance yourself from these people so you can get healthy yourself—even if it is someone whom you love very much.

- Try to be helpful to negative people. Point out the positive. Try to offer them constructive solutions, but don't let them become destructive to you.

- Be aware of how you feel after you have been in contact with certain people. Who lifts you up? Makes you laugh? Encourages you? Increase your time with these people, and decrease your time with those who bring you down.

- When faced with challenges that are very difficult, think about all the good things and the good people you have in your life. Spend time with a person who really cares about you. Remember to listen to them as well as talk about your own problems.

- Remember that you have to get along with negative people, especially at work. You might put this advice under the category "social diplomacy." "Employees who have good professional skills but do not relationally get along with co-workers, clients or management are now considered incompetent" (Teamworks Fall Newsletter, 2008). More people are terminated because of attitude-related problems than lack of job skills. Social diplomacy can take you a long way at work and in life.

> *The optimist sees opportunity in every danger; the pessimist sees danger in every opportunity.*
> —Winston Churchill

Do you use the power of positive people to improve your own attitude?

Shutterstock

CHOOSE OPTIMISM AND SURROUND YOURSELF WITH OPTIMISTIC PEOPLE

What Can I Gain by Surrounding Myself with Positive People?

Your attitude is yours. It belongs to you. You own it. Good or bad, happy or sad, optimistic or pessimistic, it is yours and you are responsible for it. However, your attitude is greatly influenced by situations in your life and by the people with whom you associate. Developing a winning, optimistic attitude can be hard, yet extremely rewarding work. Motivated and successful people have learned that one's attitude is the mirror to one's soul.

Optimism has many benefits beyond helping you develop a winning attitude. Researchers have found that people who are optimistic live longer, are more motivated, survive cancer treatment at a greater rate, have longer and more satisfying relationships, and are mentally healthier than pessimists. This would suggest that developing and maintaining a winning, optimistic attitude can help you have a longer and more satisfying quality of life.

Listen to yourself for a few days. Are you more of an optimist or a pessimist? Do you hear yourself whining, complaining, griping, and finding fault with everything and everybody around you? Do you blame others for things that are wrong in your life? Do you blame your bad grades on your professors? Is someone else responsible for your unhappiness? If these thoughts or comments are in your head, you are suffering from ***"I CAN'T" Syndrome*** (**I**rritated, **C**ontaminated, **A**ngry, **N**egative **T**houghts). This pessimistic condition can negatively influence every aspect of your life, from your self-esteem and your motivation level to your academic performance, your relationships, and your career success.

If you want to eliminate "***I CAN'T***" from your life, consider the following tips:

- Work every day to find the good in people, places, and things.
- Discover what is holding you back and what you need to push you forward.
- Visualize your success—visualize yourself actually being who and what you want to be.
- Locate and observe positive, optimistic people and things in your life.
- Make a list of who helps you, supports you, and helps you feel positive; then make a point to be around them more.
- Take responsibility for your own actions and their consequences.
- Force yourself to find five positive things a day for which to be thankful.

POSITIVE HABITS *at Work*

When you hear someone gossiping and spreading rumors, do not participate in the conversation. It can only lead to resentment and trouble. If you feel it is appropriate, say something positive about the person who is being maligned.

You've seen the difference between an optimist and a pessimist. Both are everywhere—at work, at school, and probably in your own family. Positive, upbeat, and motivated people are easy to spot. You can basically see their attitude in the way they walk, the way they carry themselves, the way they approach people, and the way they treat others. Negative people are also easy to spot—they are grouchy, late, and depressing.

Learn from both as you move through the days and months ahead. Choose your friends carefully. Seek out people who have ambition, good work habits, positive attitudes, and high ethical standards. Look for those who study hard, enjoy learning, are goal oriented, and don't mind taking a stand when they believe strongly about something. Befriend people who have interests and hobbies that are new to you. Step outside your comfort zone and add people to your circle of friends who are from a different culture, are of a different religion, or who have lived in a different geographic region. You'll be happily surprised at how much enrichment they can bring to your life and how much you grow personally and professionally in the process.

Be wary, however, of *the others*. Whiners. Degraders. Attackers. Manipulators. Pessimists. Back-stabbers. Abusers. Cowards. Two-faced racists, sexists, ageists, homophobes, ethnocentrists. These people carry around an aura so negative that it can almost be seen as a dark cloud above them. They degrade others because they do not like themselves. They find fault with everything because their own lives are unrewarding. Many of these people will do nothing to use their potential but will attack you for being motivated and trying to improve your life. We call them contaminated people.

Examine the two lists that follow. As you read through the lists, consider the people with whom you associate. Are the majority of your friends, family, peers, and work associates positive or contaminated?

Positive People:	Contaminated People:
■ Bring out the best in you	■ Bring out the worst in you
■ Find the good in bad situations	■ Find the bad in every situation
■ Are gracious and understanding	■ Are rude and uncaring
■ Build people up	■ Sabotage people, even loved ones
■ Support your dreams	■ Criticize your hopes and plans
■ Make you feel comfortable and happy	■ Make you feel uneasy, nervous, and irritable
■ Tell you the truth and offer constructive criticism	■ Are two-faced and use harsh language to "put you in your place"
■ Are open-minded and fair	■ Are narrow and ethnocentric
■ Are patient	■ Are quick to anger
■ Are giving	■ Are jealous and smothering
■ Love to learn from others	■ Think they know everything

As you think about the list above and the people in your life, ask yourself, "Do I surround myself with more positive or contaminated people?" As you consider your friends, family, class-mates, and work associates, use the space below to compare and contrast one *positive person* with one *contaminated person* in your life.

Positive Person _____

His/Her Attributes _____

_____

_____

Contaminated Person _____

His/Her Attributes _____

_____

_____

Compare and Contrast _____

_____

_____

UNDERSTAND YOUR EMOTIONAL RESPONSES

Who Pushes Your Buttons?

Should evolution be taught in the public school system? Should the drinking age be lowered to 18? Should 16-year-olds be allowed to drive? Should hate crime laws be abolished? Should same-sex couples be allowed to marry and adopt children? What emotions are you feeling right now? Did you immediately formulate answers to these questions in your mind? Do your emotions drive the way you think or act?

> *Your mentality shapes your reality.*
>
> —Bert Goldman

Emotions play a vital role in our lives. They help us feel compassion, offer assistance to others, reach out in times of need, and relate with compassion and empathy. On the other hand, our emotions can cause problems in our thinking process. They can cloud issues and distort facts. They can make us act in inappropriate ways when normally, we would not—and this can affect our performance and attitude in the workplace. Emotions are not bad—as a matter of fact, they are good and help us be human. However, it is of paramount importance that you know how to identify when your emotions are calling the shots and how to control them. You do not have to eliminate emotions from your thoughts or actions, but it is crucial that you know when your emotions are clouding an issue.

ARTICULATE YOUR HOPES AND GOALS

BIGGEST INTERVIEW *Blunders*

Rosalynn had done a very good job with her resumé and cover letter and had secured an interview with her dream company. Things got off to a good start at the interview, but Rosalynn knew she had blown it when the interviewer asked her to tell her what she knew about the company. Rosalynn realized too late that she should have made the effort to learn a great deal about the company before going to an interview!

LESSON: Always research the company and be prepared to talk about the positive things you know about it and to ask thoughtful questions. If the interviewer doesn't ask you about the company, try to find ways to weave some of your knowledge related to the company's policies into the conversation.

Where Are You Going with Your One Lifetime?

"Go tell it on the mountain, over the hills and everywhere . . . " "Why would I want to do that?" you might ask. "If I tell everyone my hopes and dreams and goals, they'll know if I don't make it." Yes, but they will also know when you do—and they can help you make it.

If others know what you want from your life or your career, they can help you bring it to fruition. When you share what type of position you want or where you would like to work, others can be on the lookout for you, and you can do the same for your peers.

Consider this: You have a secret desire to become an animation artist for Pixar Animation Studios. Yes, it is a major film company producing such hits as *Finding Nemo, Cars,* and *Toy Story.* "How stupid to think that someone from Newell, Iowa (population 887) could ever go to work for one of Disney's major studios," you might think. Wrong. Wrong. Wrong. Everyday people get fabulous dream jobs. Someone became the veterinarian for Lady Gaga's pets, someone became Oprah's personal trainer, and someone became an animator for an upcoming Disney/Pixar film. Others became the head mechanic for Delta Airlines and a chef at MGM Grand in Las Vegas, a nurse at Mercy Hospital, a firefighter for New York City, and a fashion design intern for Versace. Why? Because they had talent, they worked hard, they had a belief that they could do it, and they let others know of their hopes and dreams.

Consider this. You told your classmate that you really want to become a physical therapist. Your peer takes his mother to physical therapy one day and overhears a conversation between two staff members about an opening. She mentions this to you. You stop by the therapy center to inquire, and they are very impressed that you knew about the position and took the initiative to stop by. You fill out an application, leave your resumé, and two days later, you're called in for an interview to become an intern.

> *You are fast becoming what you are going to be.*
> —Patricia G. Moody

PUTTING IT ALL TOGETHER

A great deal of your success in the workplace depends on the characteristics and qualities you bring with you. Your attitude, optimism, and personality type will all affect your performance at work. It is important that you find good role models to emulate, that you build a strong set of values and beliefs, and that you rid yourself of negativity about yourself and others. Knowing what you want, staying focused on your goals, and working hard will be valuable assets in the workplace.

DIGITAL BRIEFCASE

Personal Branding

Review the information on personal branding on page 69. Answer the following questions as you think about creating your own brand: Me, Inc.

- What is unique about you? (Do you have special talents? Are you loyal and dedicated to your company and coworkers? Do you have unique technology talents?)
- What is a feature benefit about you? (Are you always on time? Do you deliver high-quality work? Do you get along well with team members? Are you great at problem solving?)
- What have you done that you are most proud of? (Were you on the debate team? Did you lead a team? Did you succeed at a part-time job? Did you volunteer for a charitable activity?)
- How do you sell the "sizzle" about yourself? (What can you do to be noticed and appreciated? Can you take on a project for an organization? Can you volunteer for tasks at work? Are you careful what you send out via technology that can easily be passed on to anybody else? (How about your personal advertisements when you text, e-mail, or post something to your Facebook wall? Do you stop and think before engaging in popular pastimes like "sexting?" Are you thinking when you post pictures on Facebook that might come back to haunt you later?)
- Do you volunteer or participate in things that give you power? If your meetings are disorganized, can you volunteer to write an agenda that keeps your group on track? Can you put together an informal user's group that can give you honest feedback on how your brand is doing? Ask them to give you an honest assessment of how you are perceived and what they think you need to do differently.)
- How do you measure up against four important benchmarks?
    - Are you a great team member and supportive colleague?
    - What are you a real expert at that adds value to your personal brand?

- What are you doing that adds to your ability to apply vision to everything you do?
- Are the things you are trying to accomplish practical and doable?

If you are smart, you will figure out the answer to all these questions and create a brand for which you are known, a brand that sells the best features of who you are and what you have to offer. It takes time, and it's not easy, but it is absolutely essential to your success. Know who you are! Know what you want! Build the brand that takes you there!

By thinking about who you really are, what you want, what you need, and what you have to offer an employer, you can better determine the type of position you will need in order to be happy, successful, and continue growing. If you focus on matching your vocation together with your passion, you will never face a day of "work" in your life. Work hard on developing your personal brand (Peters, 1997).

So, let's get to work on creating your personal brand.

Complete the following questions about yourself as you begin to work on developing your special brand—Me, Inc.

1. Write at least three things that you think are unique about you.

_____

_____

2. Name at least one major benefit about you.

_____

_____

3. What special talent can you add to a company's everyday function that will make you stand out?

_____

_____

4. Name something you have done that you are very proud of.

_____

_____

5. What can you do to get noticed in a subtle, positive way without appearing that you are bragging?

_____

_____

6. Do the personal messages you send reflect positively on you? Which things do you need to start doing or stop doing?

_____

_____

7. What can you volunteer to do at work or school that will give you positive visibility?

_____

_____

8. Name at least three people who can serve as your "user's group" and who will tell you honestly what you need to know and what you need to do differently.

_____

_____

_____

You should now be ready to focus on developing your brand, an important step in discovering who you are and what you have to offer.

REFERENCES

Aaker, J., & Smith, A. (2010). *The dragonfly effect.* San Francisco: Jossey-Bass.

Center for Law and Social Policy. (2003). *The language of opportunity: Expanding employment for adults with limited English skills.* Washington, DC: Author

Gordon, E. (2008). *The 2010 meltdown: Solving the impending job crisis.* Lanham, MD: Rowman & Littlefield Education.

Peters, T. (August 31, 1997). "The Brand Called You." *Fast Company.*

Teamworks Newsletter. (2008). Retrieved on March 3, 2011, from www.iwolff.com/files /teamworks/Newsletter-attitudeIsEverythingInTheWorkplace.pdf.

Tieger, P., & Barron-Tieger, B. (2001). *Do what you are: Discover the perfect career for you through the secrets of personality type* (3rd ed.). Boston: Little, Brown.

Your Personal Brand

UNIVERSITY OF
SOUTH CAROLINA
College of Hospitality, Retail
and Sport Management

Your Personal Brand: Read through the following statements with your own personal brand in mind. Answer No, Sometimes or Yes as to how you would best describe yourself today.

Am I a Great Team Member?	No	Sometimes	Yes
• Would I like to work with someone like me?		X	
• Would I like to have a team leader like me?			X
• Do I support others like they support me?			X
Am I an Expert?			
• Do people know who I am?			X
• Am I someone others seek out for advice or ideas?			X
• Is my expertise known to others?			X
• Do I continuously enhance my skills? Build on my strengths?			X
Am I a Visionary?			
• Do I have a personal vision for my life?		X	
• Have I communicated that vision to others at work? Life partner?	X		
• Do I have high standards of myself and others?		X	
Do I get results?			
• Do others call asking me how I do what I do?			X
• Am I the benchmark for my work area/pyramid?		X	
• Do I expect as much from myself as I do from others?		X	
• Do I model getting results everyday?			X
Am I Enthusiastic?			
• Do I get excited out loud? Embrace each day? Hit the floor running?			X
• Do I use a battery charger - seek out other positive people? Charge up others?			X
• Do I see life as a kid and anticipate each day?			X
• Is my attitude contagious? Is it worth catching?			X

77

Your Personal Brand

The Marnie Pearce Professionalism Program

**UNIVERSITY OF
SOUTH CAROLINA**
College of Hospitality, Retail
and Sport Management

Your Personal Brand: Read through the following words and circle the top 30 words that best describe you!

Student Name: __Delaney Wood__

(creative)	shy	(fun)	(independent)	diplomatic
extroverted	(sophisticated)	witty	dignified	satisfied
(self-reliant)	polished	calm	arrogant	confident
influential	distinctive	professional	controlled	successful
meek	(cautious)	(respectful)	(impatient)	wholesome
efficient	determined	reserved	self-centered	casual
masculine	(enthusiastic)	(approachable)	intellectual	(original)
delicate	innocent	blending	classic	savvy
(dramatic)	(controlling)	flirtatious	(active)	authoritative
restrained	severe	unique	feminine	(disciplined)
cold	(naïve)	(gentle)	(friendly)	(gracious)
fashionable	sarcastic	aggressive	elegant	persuasive
humble	attractive	stubborn	bold	(loyal)
negative	charming	(open minded)	cheerful	(precise)
(competitive)	(considerate)	harmonious	inspiring	(obedient)
sociable	receptive	cordial	daring	soft-spoken
convincing	tolerant	persistent	(optimistic)	(positive)
accurate	(restless)	(polite)	peaceful	tough
distant	(kind)	outspoken	assertive	introverted

More Descriptive Words:

Professional Summary:

TOP WORDS:
considerate
approachable
independent

disciplined
positive
optimistic

obedient
active
cautious
and
competitive

considerate
approachable
independent

disciplined
positive
competitive

LinkedIn Grading Rubric
The Marnie Pearce Professionalism Program

Presentation of Online Professional Presence: You are to have developed a LinkedIn site or other approved personal webpage. There must be no question of the quality of its representation of you as a professional in the workplace. (*If you have circumstances that would prohibit you from maintaining a current LinkedIn profile online, please contact instructor for an alternate assignment)

LinkedIn Presentation & Expectation for Participation Grade

Profile Presentation: 100 points total

- [ ] Profile picture displays you in a professional manner: **10 points**
- [ ] Invest quality time up front to create a detailed profile (connections, activities, memberships, etc.): **20 points**
- [ ] Your professional headline emphasizes any positive keywords you want to use to promote yourself: **10 points**
- [ ] Fill out the Summary field of your profile and all of your critical skills and important career-related keywords, skills section: **20 points**

- [ ] Request a connection with Mr. Collin Crick, HRSM Professional Development Instructor
- [ ] Include your professional work experience : **15 points**
- [ ] Properly represent your Education here at South Carolina: **15 points**
- [ ] Maintain a current and up-to-date profile: **10 points**

Official College of HRSM Alumni Network LinkedIn Access

- [ ] Request a connection with HRSM Alumni Director, Ms. Tina Weaver
- [ ] Completed *Personal Branding* Training in HRSM 301 Professional Development Seminar
- [ ] Completed training on *Professional Online Presence* to include LinkedIn Etiquette and Protocol
- [ ] Completed Orientation of the LinkedIn Group: Official College of HRSM Alumni Network, to include: Participation Policy, Access Process, and LinkedIn Page Review, signed/agreement by Student and Instructor.

chapter four

SOCIALIZE

PROFESSIONAL DRESS AND DINING WITH CLASS

Never go to bed at night wondering if you were a conversational gun in the slandering of a person's character or the endangerment of his/her future.
—Letitia Baldridge

PERFECT YOUR PROFESSIONAL IMAGE

How Do You Dress and Dine to Be Remembered for All the Right Reasons?

Should I use the shortest fork for my appetizer or the salad? Should I wear French cuffs on an interview? Should I extend my hand to be shaken or wait until a hand is offered?

Many people have the mistaken idea that everyone knows how to dress, how to dine properly, and how to demonstrate good manners. Some even believe that these qualities are not important. The truth is that these things are not taught at home as much as they once were, and many people grow up not knowing these basic points. However, do not be mistaken—first impressions, manners, etiquette, and basic grooming remain very important.

Several years ago, John Malloy, an "image guru," said, "As much as one-third of your success depends on what you wear." In Malloy's opinion, your appearance, image, and presence contribute greatly to your overall success in your career. When you combine a powerful first impression, professional dress, good basic manners, excellent dining etiquette, proper language skills, and add a winning smile, you have all the makings of an outstanding professional package. More and more colleges and schools are providing educational experiences in all these areas for their students. The professional package is the "icing on the cake" that helps students secure the job they want and then move up rapidly in the ranks.

What Is Image, Exactly?

What do we mean by image? And why do you have to have one? Image is the mental picture that people have of you when you pass through their minds. Image is what people see when they think of you. Whether you like it or not, you have an image. Take a minute right now if you can, and go stand in front of a full-length mirror. Pretend this person who is looking back at you is someone other than you. Try to look at your image with an unbiased eye. What do you see? Are you dressed well? Are you clean and pressed? Does your hair look well groomed? Are you smiling? Are your clothes altered correctly and professionally? Do you think you present an upper-middle-class image? If not, you have work to do, because image has a great deal to do with how people treat you and respect you.

Your image and attire combine to make up one component of your overall ability to practice good judgment. You want to dress like you have good judgment and demonstrate an image that

makes people look at you as a professional. Knowing how to dress for work can be challenging and confusing. Because dressing can be daunting, many people, especially women, fail at making the right selections.

First, you should determine if your company has a dress code. If so, get a copy from your HR department and abide by the policies. Second, consider your long-term career goals and dress for the position you aspire to rather than the one you are in today. Third, pay attention to how the company leaders dress and take your cue from this group of successful people. Fourth, determine if your position dictates what you wear. If you are in accounting, for example, you might need to wear dark suits, blazers, and other professional outfits. Finally, consider your business wardrobe an investment. It should last for years if you buy classic clothing and avoid putting too much money into fads.

Dress to Impress

Many people like to demonstrate their own style and pay little attention to what constitutes appropriate dress at work. Frequently, companies today don't spell out exactly what they are looking for in employee dress, so you need to pay attention to what the successful people are wearing. Even if you are required to wear a uniform, notice how others present themselves. Is the uniform clean and pressed? Does it fit well?

You have to be able to determine for yourself what looks good on you, what is over-the-top dressing for your particular environment, and what is considered dress that will impress your superiors, colleagues, and customers. Look carefully at the people who have already made it and those who appear to be on a fast track. What do they wear to work? Are they overly casual? Do they wear jeans to work on casual day? Do you see any of them with earrings, tongue studs, or bright red streaks in their hair? Do you find any who have tattoos on their necks, heads, and other conspicuous places? Companies are hiring you to represent them, and they want a positive appearance from all their employees. The appearance that was appropriate at school and in a casual environment may not be acceptable in the work environment.

Women's Dress

Women have so many more choices than men—and so many more ways to get it right or wrong. Getting it right can be a great asset to someone thinking about promotions or making positive impressions. You have many choices that can complement your individual style and body type and still present you in a positive light. You should use dress to reinforce how serious you are about your work and your career.

Whatever your profession, you want to look the part. You don't necessarily want to wear clothes that make you stand out; rather, you want to look good so that people will respond to you appropriately. The mark of a well-dressed woman is that she always looks professional and well-dressed, but you don't necessarily remember exactly what she had on. If you stand out, you have to be sure it is for the right reasons—perhaps a flair for color, style, jewelry, or the ability to mix styles.

If you need to (or are required to) wear business suits, they should be dark colors and preferably should be natural fabrics like wool or linen. Shoes should be stylish, but comfortable, preferably leather, and jewelry should be well-made, preferably gold or silver. Women's professional shoes should not have open heels or toes, straps, platforms, or high spike heels.

Clothes should always be cleaned, pressed and immaculate—no spots, safety pins, or hems or cuffs that are in bad repair. Purses and belts should be leather and in good repair. Your blouses should be tailored; you should avoid busy prints, frilly lace, and sexy garments. Likewise, you should avoid pastel colors for major pieces of your wardrobe, especially light pink (which screams "baby girl") and bright, garish colors. Appearance is a cultivated practice, and you can learn to look and act successful, which will go a long way toward making you successful. To get an idea of how people dress in your profession, purchase magazines or journals that have pictures of people who work in your profession. You might also consider visiting an office where you would like to work and observing the dress of the women who work there. You want to have an image that says "understated elegance."

Although pants are acceptable in most business offices, women should typically stick to pantsuits that have matching blazer and pants. The pants should be hemmed at the proper length according to what is in style. Sleeves should be hemmed so they do not extend below the wrist. Most clothes require some alterations. Avoid buying clothes off the rack that do not fit well or wearing them without having them altered properly to fit you. No matter what salespeople tell you, clothes off the rack almost always need alterations.

The information presented previously primarily relates to business dress for women who are working in business offices. Naturally, if you are working in aviation mechanics, you can't wear pumps and a business suit. Likewise, if you are working in a cubicle as a computer programmer, you will find that most of your colleagues aren't wearing dark business suits. Some positions,

Shutterstock

If you saw this person at lunch, would she impress you as a professional?

> *Fashions fade, style is eternal.*
> — *Yves Saint Laurent*

such as nursing, will require you to wear a uniform. When it comes to dress in non-traditional fields and fields other than business, you should observe what others in your position or department are wearing and follow suit. No matter what your position or dress code, you should always wear clean, pressed clothes in good repair. Some universal dress tips are presented in Figure 4.1.

Your image should match your ambitions. If you were going to work today, would your wardrobe reflect your ambitions? Would you look chic and stylish, or would you appear frumpy and nondescript? Would you look like a student or like a professional? What would people say about your grooming? What does your body language say about you? Image is a complete package, and anyone can improve personal image. Some people are naturally more attractive than others, and some are more graceful and charming, but anyone can learn to develop presence and build a better image.

Figure 4.1 Universal Dress Tips for Women in a Business Office Environment

Remember that you cannot be sexy and professional in the same outfit—so make up your mind what you want to be known for. No one will take you seriously if you dress provocatively at work.

- The best colors for business suits are navy, black, gray, burgundy, olive, tan, and khaki.

- Pantsuits should preferably have a matching blazer and pants, should be hemmed to the right length, and should never be too short.

- Sleeves should be hemmed so they do not extend below the wrist.

- If you wear a skirt, it should come at least to the top of your knees, even if very short skirts are in style—fashions may dictate changes in skirt lengths, but they should never be too short at work. When you sit, your thighs should be covered.

- Business dresses and pantsuits are fine for most days, but if you have an important meeting, wear a business suit with a skirt. If you wear a dress, wear a blazer or jacket over it.

- Your clothing should not be louder than your voice or personality.

- Avoid overpowering perfume that may be offensive to others. Some people are allergic to strong perfumes.

- Your hair should be clean, well-groomed, and fashionable and should not distract from your overall appearance.

- Avoid clothes that are too tight, see-through, or have long slits in the front that expose too much leg.

- Have your clothes altered to fit well.

- Avoid all extremes such as trendy clothes; bleached hair; or unnatural hair colors such as green, blue, or bright red streaks.

- Have no visible tattoos.

- Avoid any kind of body piercings that are obvious, especially facial piercings or multiple earrings.

- Jewelry should be simple—gold or silver is best.

- Wear no more than one ring on each hand, except for wedding and engagement rings.

- A nice gold watch and one bracelet are nice touches at work.

- Hose should coordinate with your outfit, but usually a barely black or suntan color works for most business occasions. You should always wear hose in the winter.

- Avoid colored, fishnet, and patterned hose at work.

- Carry a cordovan briefcase and no purse so you don't look like a pack horse when you go to an important meeting.

- Carry a briefcase or leather portfolio even if you have nothing in it. It is the image you are going for—a professional with her accessories.

- If you carry a purse, organize it, and don't be seen digging around in it searching for an item.

- Walk briskly and act like you know where you are going. Never drag around at work. This behavior becomes part of your image.

Women: Considering all the tips for dress and image improvement that we have shared with you, list several things about your typical dress that you think you could (and should) improve so that your appearance more closely matches that of your potential coworkers and your career goals.

_____

_____

_____

_____

_____

_____

Men's Dress

One of the best ways for men to stand out is by dressing in an outstanding manner. The typical male does not give a great deal of attention to his appearance, so when a man does it right, he gets a lot of positive attention. As stated earlier, women have many more choices than men—and many more ways of making bad decisions. Any man can become a very good dresser if he is willing to work at it.

While you may not work in a job that requires a suit, you need at least one nice suit and preferably two, especially for the interview. You want interviewers to think they are getting a bargain in you. The best times for men to buy suits are after Christmas and after the Fourth of July, when most nice mens stores put their suits on sale. You might also look for warehouse sales, which often provide excellent bargains if you know how to shop for them.

Many suits can be worn year-round, except perhaps on the coldest or hottest days. If you live in the South or Southwest, you don't need heavy wool clothes — you will get very little wear from them. Regardless of where you live, however, the labels in your suits should contain wool because it helps suits keep their shape better after cleaning. If you are taking a traveling position, you need clothes that won't wrinkle badly.

Certainly, the rules of dress for a business office do not apply to many professional careers such as plumbing, electrical engineering, auto mechanics, computer programming, and medical assistant positions. In such positions, men should observe what others at their level are wearing and dress accordingly. If you are a computer programmer, for example, you may be allowed to wear jeans and a golf shirt. If this is the case, be sure your jeans are clean, pressed, and do not have holes or frayed cuffs, even if this is a fashion statement.

Review the tips for men's dress presented in Figure 4.2.

Dress for interviews should be based on the kind of job you for which are interviewing. If you are dressing to be machine technician, you would dress differently from someone interviewing for a position in allied health. "The first judgment an interviewer makes is going to be based on how you look and what you are wearing" (Doyle, 2011).

Shutterstock

Do you think a company would be interested in hiring this man?

Figure 4.2 Universal Dress Tips for Men in a Business Office Environment

- If you are going to work in a company where you need to wear suits, start building a good wardrobe now. Suits and blazers are expensive and should be accumulated over a period of time.

- Most men need to own at least two suits—navy and charcoal gray work well for most men and fit in well in most companies.

- As a new graduate, you can interview in a blue blazer and charcoal gray slacks if you don't have a suit. A nice sport coat is a good wardrobe addition.

- If you are required to wear dress shirts to work, you should own at least 6–10 of them, including several white shirts and at least two light blue shirts. French blue is also a versatile color that can be worn with most of the colors mentioned above. Of course, you can gradually accumulate this collection.

- The only color shirt to wear to an interview is white, and it should be starched and immaculate.

- Dress shirts should be starched—always! Do not rely on permanent pressed because they always look unkempt if not pressed.

- Dress shirts should always be long-sleeved, even in the summer. Never wear short-sleeved dress shirts—especially to an interview!

- A small monogram on your left cuff is a nice touch.

- You might want to consider at least one shirt with French cuffs and cufflinks.

- Suits should either be two- or three-button. Stay away from trendy suits that will go out of style soon.

- Purchase black and brown belts and shoes; they will look good with almost everything.

- The dressiest shoe a man can wear is a lace-up wing-tip, but young men can wear tasseled loafers or cap-toe lace-up shoes just as well. If you don't understand these terms, ask a shoe salesperson to explain them to you.

- Heels of shoes should not look worn, and shoes should always be polished and shined.

- Socks should be black if worn with gray, navy, or black. Bare leg should not show if you cross your legs, so buy long socks.

- Never wear white socks with a business suit or sport coat. Patterned socks are the mark of a well-dressed man if they are coordinated well.

- Ties should be stylish and bought with careful consideration. If you don't know how to choose a tie, get help from a salesperson at a nice men's store. Unless she has excellent taste, don't let your girlfriend or your wife choose your ties.

- Ties should be made of silk in a stylish width and should have no spots on them.

- Men should learn to tie a knot that is in style. The bottom part of the tie should reach right below your belt. Do not wear a tie that sits on your stomach and indicates that you do not know how to dress professionally.

- Men should wear a mild, non-offensive cologne.

- Remove fat wallets, large key rings, and excessive change from your pockets. You want to look streamlined and put together.

- Buy a nice leather briefcase, and use it even if you have nothing in it but your lunch!

GRADUATE *Quote*

Jonathan T. Ellis
Graduate!
The University of South Carolina, Columbia, SC
Career: Network Administrator, The University of South Carolina

The most important lesson I learned was this: Perfect your capacity to articulate your abilities and skills because you never know what employers are really looking for. Never be discouraged. Your dream position is out there.

Men: Considering all the tips we have discussed with you, list several things about your dress that you think you could (and should) improve so your dress more closely matches that of your potential coworkers and your career goals.

_____

_____

_____

_____

_____

_____

Business Casual—The Type of Professional Dress That Stumps Many Men and Women

The important thing to remember about business casual is this: "While casual may be optional, looking professional is not. Exercising poor work attire choices can convey an unfavorable message to your superiors and colleagues and ultimately stunt your growth within an organization" (Zuri, 2011). Business casual should be crisp, clean, neat, and pressed. You should feel well-dressed even if you bump into the president.

Many businesses allow employees to "dress down," especially on Friday. Dressing down does not mean "anything goes." Some people really mess up with casual dress, and they stand out for all the wrong reasons because they don't take it seriously enough.

Although you don't want to overdress when others are casual, you don't want to go to great extremes with your casual dress either. Actually, it is just as expensive to dress well for casual occasions as it is to dress for business—and more difficult for many people because they fail to take it seriously. A general rule of thumb for dressing for success is this: Observe what others, including your supervisors, are wearing.

Some basic tips for business casual dress are listed below:

- On casual days, men should wear a good pair of dress slacks and a golf shirt or a knit shirt with a blazer.
- Men can also wear a button-down shirt with slacks and a blazer. Women can wear simple slacks that are pressed, the right length, and not too tight.
- Under no circumstances should you wear t-shirts and wrinkled khakis or unpressed jeans. Tennis shoes, sandals, or hiking boots are never appropriate.
- Showing cleavage for women is never appropriate, no matter what you see on television or in magazines.
- Facial hair should be worn only if higher-ranking company executives do so, and should be well-groomed.

Shutterstock

Does this man pass the test as a well-dressed professional?

■ Makeup should be conservative and natural looking. Nails should be groomed and cleaned. Women should avoid very bright polish for business. Likewise, they should avoid all the fashion design nails done by salons for work.

DINE WITH CLASS

Who Cares If I Don't Use the Right Fork?

The mark of a very polished person is the ability to use outstanding dining etiquette, to order food and beverage with confidence. The finer points of dining etiquette need to be studied and used as you enter your career and consider moving up. No one is exempt from needing to know how to sit and eat a meal with dignity and grace. No one! Read a good etiquette book and take it seriously. Research shows that only about 12 percent of new hires are skilled in the social graces. In fact, many companies hire consultants to teach their employees how to practice good etiquette. Etiquette or the lack of it may mean the difference between success or failure. Excellent manners will set you apart early in your career. Manners will also make a positive impression on almost everyone, especially your customers and clients!

We assume you know the basics, such as chew with your mouth closed, keep your elbows off the table, pass food to the right, cut your meat only one piece at a time, and butter only one small piece of bread at a time—but many people don't know these rules! You also need to know the following basic rules of good etiquette and dining:

Shutterstock

Do these employees look dressed professionally for work on business casual day?

■ A utensil that has been used should never be placed on a tablecloth. Place it on the edge of your plate.

■ If you use a sweetener or other item that has been wrapped in paper, slip the paper under your bread plate. Don't leave it on the table in a conspicuous manner.

■ Remember LR, LR, LR—liquids to the right. This means that you should only drink from or use the glasses on your right. Solids, such as bread plates, are always on your left.

■ As part of your interview, you may be taken to a nice restaurant. People will be observing to determine if you can represent them well.

■ Order something that is easy to eat and not the most expensive thing on the menu. A good rule is to follow the price range of the host who is taking you to dinner.

■ Avoid messy foods. Spaghetti is difficult to manage, soup might drip on your clothes, and ribs can't be eaten easily.

■ If you eat soup, dip your spoon away from you, rather than towards you.

■ Do not push food onto your fork with your knife or a piece of bread.

■ If the host orders dessert, you can do so, but you should not if he or she does not.

■ Under no circumstances should you drink or smoke, even if others at the table do. If your host orders wine, you may have one glass of wine if you would like to, but you should not have any more.

■ If you share foods—and this is not advised on an interview—do not pass your plate back and forth. Using a clean, unused utensil, place a portion on your bread plate and pass it to the person for whom it is intended or ask your server for a small plate.

Figure 4.3 is a diagram of a formal table setting. Study it carefully so you will know what to do if you are dining at a formal restaurant. Starting at the outer edge, use the appropriate fork with each course. Again, the rule to remember is: Solids on the left, liquids on the right; in other words, your personal bread plate is on the upper left hand side of your plate, and your drink will be on the right. If you can't remember this, wait and watch others at the table, then do what they do.

If you leave the table, place your napkin on your chair; do not put it on the table until the meal has been completed and you are leaving the restaurant. When you finish your meal and are leaving the table, fold your napkin loosely and place it back on the table.

When women approach or leave the table, men should stand. If it is a business occasion, women should stand at the beginning of the meal and shake hands as the men are doing. Women do not need to stand when someone leaves the table or returns. A man should help the woman to his right with her chair and then help the woman on his left if no one else is doing so. Take your seat from the right side of the chair.

You may be saying to yourself, "Who cares?" or "What difference does it make which fork I use?" The answer is simple and complex—no one and everyone. However, consider this: It is always better to have knowledge and skills and not need them than to need them and not have them. You will use this often!

There is much to learn en route to developing a professional presence, and you might make some mistakes. Learn from them and keep working until you are comfortable in any setting.

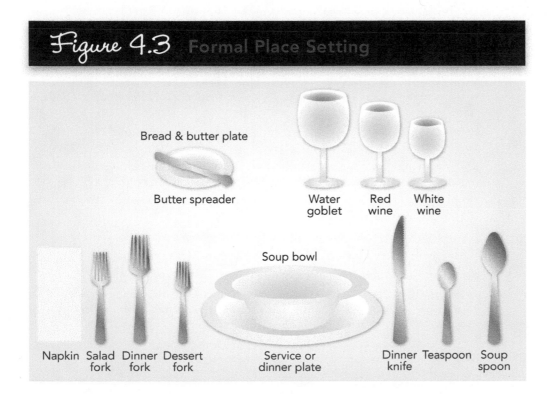

Figure 4.3 Formal Place Setting

REFERENCES

Behind bars II: Substance abuse and America's prison population. (2011). Retrieved May 14, 2011, from www.casacolumbia.org/templates/PressReleases.aspx?articleid=592&zoneid=79.

Buddy, T. (2011). Substance abuse in the workplace: A dangerous and expensive problem. Retrieved June 2, 2011, from http://alcoholism.about.com/cs/work/a/aa990120.htm.

Cooper, M. (2002). Alcohol use and risky sexual behavior among college students and youth. *Journal of Studies on Alcohol, 63*(2), 101.

Daly, K., & Richards, J. (2007). Substance abuse. Retrieved July 18, 2011, from www .emedicinehealth.com/substanceabuse/articleem.htm.

Doyle, A. (2010). How to dress for an interview. Retrieved July 18, 2011, from http:// jobsearch.about.com/od/interviewattire/a/interviewdress.htm.

Hoffman, J., & Froemke, S. (2007). *Addiction: Why can't they just stop?* Emmaus, PA: Rodale.

Kersten, D. (2002). Office romances can be risky. USA TODAY. Retrieved July 21, 2011, from www.usatoday.com/money.jobcenter/workplace/relationships/2002-11-12-office-romance.

Taylor, D. (2005). The intuitive life blog. "Why are office romances such a bad idea?" Retrieved May 18, 2011, from http://www.intuitive.com/blog/why_are_office_romances_such_a_bad_idea.html

Vault.com. (2010). Office Romance Survey 2010. Retrieved May 19, 2011, from www.vault .com/wps/portal/usa/vcm/detail/Career-Advice/Office-Romance/Office-Romance-Survey-2010?id=5519&filter_type=0&filter_id=0

Zuri, I. (2011). How to dress for work for women. Retrieved May 15, 2011, from www.ehow .com/how6223951dress-work-women.html#ixzz1MQBf9L4M.

Professional Attire

The Marnie Pearce Professionalism Program

1. Identify personal characteristics to effectively interact with internal and external environments.

2. Develop a professional attitude and image.

3. Design a strategic career plan and create necessary documents to obtain career goals.

Professional Attire

Men's Interview Attire:

Men's Business Professional:

Men's Business Casual:

Women's Interview Attire:

Women's Business Professional:

Women's Business Casual:

Printed Name_____

chapter five

CHANGE

DIRECTING YOUR LIFE THROUGH CONTINUOUS POSITIVE CHANGE

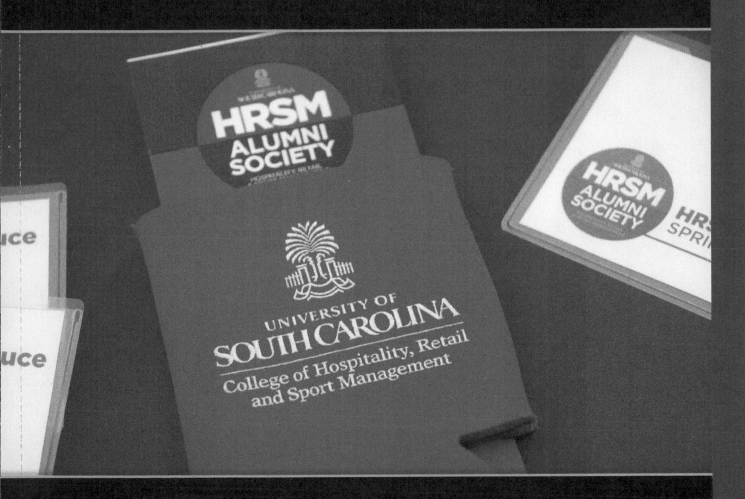

*We cannot become what we are capable
of being by remaining who we are.*
—Unknown

YOU ARE ON YOUR WAY

How Do You Plan to G4I (Go for It)?

Once you get a position and begin to prove yourself in this new job, you need to think about long-range plans, thriving in your career, and making a name for yourself as a hard-working, creative team player. There are many ways to do this. Of course, the most important thing you need to do is to excel at the entry-level job you accept in the beginning. You may not like some of the menial tasks assigned to you, and in your heart, you may know that you can do bigger and better things. The fact remains, however, that if you don't do this first job well, there won't be any promotions. So you need to start strong and never let up. Start strong and finish stronger! You should do everything possible to be a good colleague who gets along well with everyone. But this doesn't mean you can't simultaneously plan and strategize to move up the ladder, get a position with more authority and higher pay, and gain recognition for your accomplishments. The best way to make this happen is to plan for it. As you have already learned, you need short-term and long-term goals, you need to brand yourself, and you also need a career plan.

As you mature and gain confidence, your priorities and interests will change. When you begin working in your first job, you may be willing to go anywhere and explore the world. At certain times in your career, you may welcome change, and at others, you may just want things to hold steady. "At some stages, there are likely to be significant pressures on your career due to family commitments" (Eby, Casper, Lockwood, Bordeaux, and Brinley, 2005). For now, you need to focus first on the job at hand while looking down the road at where you want your career to go. So what do you need to do besides doing a good job right out of the gate? In this chapter, we will provide many ways you can make a name for yourself, find rewards inside and outside of work, build your personal brand, continue learning and growing—and most importantly, continue changing.

You will learn soon enough that you are responsible for you. Even if you have an excellent mentor and supportive network, you are still in charge of your life, and it's basically up to you to make things happen. You may encounter many people who are willing to help you, but no one is going to make things happen in your career but you. While doing a good job is imperative, working hard by itself may not get you ahead. Haven't you known people who worked hard all their lives and never really got ahead? We will show you how to work hard and smart and to embrace change as a natural part of your life.

Previously, we asked you to set goals and to know what you want. This chapter is about doing the extras, taking the next step, going out of your way, giving back to others, and finding many ways to grow and expand your potential so you can accomplish your goals and dreams. It is designed to help you focus more attention on your own personal brand and to learn to gain positive visibility that can help you earn promotions and respect. And most of all, it is about embracing change, taking risks, and never looking back. It's about getting ready to G4I!

> It is not the strongest of the species that survive, nor the most intelligent, but the one most responsive to change.
>
> —Charles Darwin

> Choose to be happy!
>
> —Michael J. Fox

ACCEPTING CHANGE AS A NATURAL PART OF LIFE

How Can I Learn to Embrace Change When It Scares Me to Death?

Change is the one constant that you can expect when you go to work. It is a myth that change will go away! Most people are afraid of change, even good change, because they are leaving their comfort zone. It is much less frightening to us if we just keep going on the way we are. The good news is that you can learn strategies for accepting change and making positive things happen. Choose to be a navigator of change rather than a victim.

You will probably hear the term *paradigm* used in the workplace. A paradigm is simply a way of doing things—it's a pattern and a system of how things are working right now. A *paradigm shift* is a rapid change from doing things one way to a totally new way—it's a transformation or a revolution. Paradigm shifts don't just happen; they are usually driven by a leader or a management team that shakes things up. When people are heavily invested in an old paradigm and have worked hard to get to this position, they are very likely to resist the new paradigm. You can't afford to be one of these people.

When a company makes a paradigm shift, there is usually a good reason: The competition is getting keener; the global economy is putting pressure on production; or the old ways are simply not working anymore. If the leader of the company or your division wants to change, you need to help make his or her ideas work. If you embrace change, you will become a navigator of change; if you reject it, you will become a victim. Change is coming! How you deal with it is up to you.

DRIVERS, DODGERS, AND DEFEATISTS

Which Will You Become?

When we are faced with rapid change or a dramatic loss of some kind, people become **drivers**, **dodgers**, or **defeatists**. Drivers make up their minds to embrace the change that has come their way and take control by driving their own lives and decisions. Others, dodgers, dodge the change and just let life happen to them; still others, the defeatists, let hard times and rapid change defeat them.

How you deal with change is in your hands. You can choose to be a driver or you can choose to be a defeatist. A great deal of how you become a driver rather than a dodger or defeatist will depend on your attitude. Study Figure 5.1 for traits that explain each category.

STRATEGIES FOR DEALING WITH CHANGE

How Can I Practice Carpe Mañana?

You might ask, "What in the world is **carpe mañana?**" You have probably heard of carpe diem, which means "seize the day." Carpe mañana means "seize tomorrow." That term probably describes better than anything what we want you to be prepared to do after reading and studying this chapter. We want you to learn to work hard and smart today as you prepare for more success tomorrow. In the world we live in, you cannot afford to be focused only on today.

Figure 5.1 Drivers, Dodgers, or Defeatists

Drivers	Dodgers	Defeatists
Realize that change is coming and they can't stop it. They know that to reduce their personal anxiety, they have to go to work and embrace the changes.	Try to pretend that they are accepting change but secretly work against it; they may feel entitled to having things stay the same because they have been there a long time.	Are frequently scared and uneasy and afraid of what is coming; will say things like "We are doing fine. Why do we need to change?" or "We've never done this before." Uncertainty breeds fear.
Are genuinely excited about the changes that are happening and the new opportunities it presents for their career.	Are only focused on themselves and no one else or the company; worry about their job changing; wonder if they will have to do more work or a job they don't like.	Think the world is against them and their boss is out to get them; fear losing control over their work or personal situation; worry about losing status that they have gained in the past.
Try to learn everything they can about where the organization is headed so they can participate in leading change; anticipate change.	Complain a lot and try to undercut the boss without being open about it while secretly hoping things will stay the same.	Usually openly resist change and try to stop it by sabotaging ideas; pull back; undercut the boss with negative remarks and actions.
Think about ways change can enhance their personal career; attack the future instead of protecting the past.	Are passive-aggressive in many ways; make no efforts to embrace change or to lead.	Many times leave their job voluntarily or are among the first to be downsized because they have shown they cannot or will not change.

Life seems to just serve up change, ready or not. It is simply a part of life. Change happens, and with it comes some level of discomfort, but what change does to you is really up to you. We tend to pay more attention to bad or disastrous change than we do to things that actually bring us joy and happiness. In addition to being prepared for difficult change, we need to prepare for joyful change, and we need to set ourselves up to have joy and happiness in our lives. Abraham

G R A D U A T E *Quote*

Zack Karper
Honor Graduate!
The Art Institute of Philadelphia
Career: Head of Video Production
buggleproductions.com, Dream Camp Foundation

The biggest lesson that I learned in college was to treat every project, whether a paper, a speech, or a film, as if it was your baby. Nurture it. Care for it. Feed it. Make it great and never raise it halfway. Give your baby your all. Today, as head of video production at Buggle Productions, I live my dream of working in film and I get to help troubled kids who were in the same shoes I was in. I get to make a difference. If you work hard and put 100 percent into your projects, you will get to help people, too.

Figure 5.2 How to Practice Carpe Mañana When Dealing with Change

- Focus on carpe mañana, which means "seize tomorrow." Don't allow yourself to get comfortable with what is happening today. Be prepared for what is coming by making yourself better. *Prepare* is a keyword for being able to deal with change of any kind. Anticipate!

- Practice *kaizen*, a Japanese term that means "continuous improvement," by doing little things better and by setting and achieving increasingly higher standards.

- Face change by embracing it—good or bad—and look for the new opportunities that change brings. View change as growth. You cannot get better unless you change.

- Deal with change by understanding its phases:
  - Denial (includes focusing on the past, apathy, withdrawal)
  - Resistance (includes blame, anxiety, depression)
  - Adaptation (includes loss of energy, confusion, frustration, and beginning to adjust)
  - Commitment (includes clearer focus, new ideas, working better with others)

- When dealing with change, we encourage you to move up to the next level—create. In other words, make things happen; don't just accept things as they are. Turn the challenge of change into a positive. What new opportunities does change bring for you?

- If change puts everyone back at zero, seize the opportunity! You now have a level playing field with other employees who have been there a long time. Make the most of it!

- Associate with people who are embracing change, not resisting it. You want to be seen as a navigator, not a victim. Avoid those who are negative and pulling back. They will be among the first to go.

- Look for the signs of change so you are not shocked when they happen. Try to spot trends. Don't bury your head in the sand and keep doing the same things you have always done. Is the company changing leadership? Is the stock doing well? Are factories moving overseas? In the old days of chariot warfare, a dust storm was an indication of an approaching enemy. Do you see the dust storms before they engulf you?

- Think differently—obviously, things are changing in your company, or they should be. In what ways is your company changing and how do you fit in better? Help create value by making yourself useful and available to try new things.

- Revise your personal budget and save more money so you can survive a loss of job or any other bad event; increase your cash reserves; and reduce your debt.

- Reach out to friends and your support system for help during difficult changes, such as loss of job, death of a family member, or a painful divorce, but do not overburden them by focusing on your problems all the time. Seek professional counseling if you are severely depressed.

- Avoid negative coping mechanisms such as alcohol, denial, overeating, blaming, passiveness, and revenge. All of these just make a bad situation worse.

- Begin today to look down the road and try to figure out what is happening next. How can you learn strategies that help you "leapfrog" over people who are sitting still and pulling back and refusing to change?

- Ask yourself these questions on a regular basis: "How do I span the distance between what I am today and what I want to become? How do I continue to make the right changes that promote growth and success?"

- Keep moving! Exercise to remove stress from your body. Do not lie on the couch and watch endless television. Convert fear into energy! Get out of the ditch of depression and up on the road, where you are in the driver's seat. If you want milk, go find a cow instead of waiting for the cow to find you.

- Balance yourself. Find ways to bring joy into your life. Simplify your life. Take care of yourself and those whom you love.

Lincoln said, "We are just about as happy as we make up our minds to be." We need to make up our minds to be happy and joyful and to deal with what comes our way.

No matter how optimistic and prepared we are, however, some bad things are going to happen to us. This kind of change may take more time to work through, but there are special ways of coping with difficult changes. Since you know change will always be coming, you can always be prepared, to some extent, to deal with it. To prepare for change, you have to have a good attitude, you must be flexible, and you have to be optimistic that you can handle it. Having a positive self-worth is very important to being able to deal with change. Figure 5.2 provides some ways for handling change effectively.

SKILLS AND ABILITIES VALUED BY EMPLOYERS

Do You Have the Right Stuff?

As you begin to map out your career plan, you need to give careful attention to certain skills that employers value highly. Although some positions require very specific job skills and knowledge, almost all jobs today require a set of universally sought-after skills. These skills can be developed if you are missing some, but it is important to be able to showcase all of them on your resumé. Figure 5.3 is a list of the top 10 skills most valued by employers (ASVAB, 2009).

As you can see, all these skills can be developed. You have to be honest with yourself and identify the ones you need to work on most. So exactly what do employers want in each of these categories?

What Employers Are Saying

According to the report *College Learning for the New Global Century* (Association of American Colleges and Universities, 2007), "Employers want college graduates to acquire versatile knowledge and skills. Fully sixty-three percent of employers believe that too many recent college graduates do not have the skills they need to succeed in the global economy and a majority of employers believe that only half or fewer recent graduates have the skills or knowledge needed to advance or to be promoted in their companies."

Shutterstock

Have you ever used negative coping mechanisms? If so, what did you learn?

Figure 5.3 Skills Highly Valued by Employers

Review the list. Then rank the skills from 1–10 by each skill according to which ones you think are most highly valued.

Analytical skills	_____	Interpersonal skills	_____
Communication skills	_____	Problem-solving skills	_____
Computer skills	_____	Strong work ethic	_____
Flexibility/Adaptability	_____	Teamwork skills	_____
Initiative	_____	Technical skills	_____

Once you have ranked the skills, check them against the answers that were most selected by participants in the survey, which are provided below.

Skills Rank

1. Communication skills
2. Strong work ethic
3. Teamwork skills
4. Initiative
5. Analytical skills
6. Computer skills
7. Flexibility/Adaptability
8. Interpersonal skills
9. Problem-solving skills
10. Technical skills

> *Life is about change, and about movement and about being something other than what you are at this very moment.*
>
> —Oprah Winfrey

Whether we like it or not, a massive transformation is going on all around us in this country, as well as all over the world. Thriving in the coming years is going to be more difficult than in the past and will require certain new and different abilities and attitudes to be successful. You will need to learn the skills that will make you competitive, give you an edge, and help you master a life filled with changes and challenges.

Many of these skills are outlined in the following section. These skills will be needed for your success, personal independence, and growth in the new economy. Study them carefully, as each one will help you create a positive transition to the world of work.

CORNERSTONES FOR SUCCESS IN A CHANGING WORLD

What Major Skills Do I Need to Be Successful on the Job?

SEEK EXCELLENCE AS A COMMUNICATOR.   Writing, speaking, and listening skills are constantly listed by employers as mandatory for success in any profession. Few people actually possess these qualities—especially all three. If you want to put yourself ahead of the competition, enroll in classes, attend seminars, join Toastmasters—anything that will help you learn more effective writing, speaking, and listening skills.

BECOME A SOUGHT-AFTER EMPLOYEE.   A strong work ethic is another valuable quality that sets you apart from the other job seekers. A work ethic can include a variety of characteristics, including your pride, passion, professionalism, ability to work on a team, and ability to adapt, grow, and change. Your work ethic is how you perform at work without a job description, constant supervision, or someone threatening you. Your work ethic is not tied to what you do to get a raise or a promotion, but rather what you do because it is the right thing to do. In today's work environment, employers want to make sure that you are dedicated to your job, your company, and your colleagues.

Shutterstock

Are your communication skills an asset or a liability?

PRACTICE LOYALTY AND TRUSTWORTHINESS. Loyalty to your employer is a highly valued trait. However, one's loyalty cannot be measured by a resumé or determined by a simple interview. Proving that you have the characteristics of loyalty and trustworthiness comes over time. It may take years to establish loyalty and trustworthiness with your company and within your industry, but with hard work, dedication, and honesty, it can and will be achieved. Be forewarned, however. While it takes years to build trust, it only takes seconds to destroy it.

ACT WITH CONFIDENCE AND MAKE BOLD DECISIONS. Appropriate confidence and boldness are important to employers. There is a difference between having confidence in yourself, your work, and your decision-making ability and being "cocky." Confidence comes from experience, calculated risk taking, and previous successes. Employers are looking for confident people who are not afraid to make hard decisions. They are also seeking individuals who have confidence through experience. There is a difference between bragging about doing something and actually doing it. There is a difference between being hard and making hard decisions.

USE CRITICAL-THINKING SKILLS. The ability to think your way through problems and challenges is highly valued by employers. Employers are looking for people who can distinguish fact from opinion; identify fallacies; analyze, synthesize, and determine the value of a piece of information; think beyond the obvious; see things from varying angles; and arrive at sound solutions. They also want people who possess the emotional intelligence to critically and creatively work to resolve challenges.

MANAGE YOUR PRIORITIES WELL. Setting priorities and managing time are essential to success in today's stressful workplace. Today, maybe more than any other time in mankind's history, we are faced with more and more to do and what seems like less and less time in which to do it. Your success depends on how well you manage your priorities, both personally and professionally. Priority management not only involves getting today's work accomplished, it also involves the ability to plan for your personal and professional future. Use your time wisely at work, at home, and in leisure.

MULTIPLY BY MULTITASKING. The ability to multitask, or accomplish several things at once, will serve you well in the workplace and at home. A recent newspaper cartoon suggested that you are too busy if you are multitasking in the shower. This may be true, but in keeping pace with today's workforce, this is another essential task—the ability to do more than one thing at a time, and the ability to do them all very well. If you have not had much experience in multitasking, we suggest that you begin slowly. Don't take on too many things at one time. As you understand more about working on and completing several tasks at a time, you can expand your abilities in this arena. An example of multitasking at home is to have a casserole baking while clothes are washing at the same time you are researching a project on the Internet. To be successful in today's fast-paced world, you must be able to manage several tasks at once—without burning dinner.
Shutterstock

STAY CURRENT AND BUILD TRANSFERABLE SKILLS. Keeping your skills and knowledge current is essential to your success. Building skills that can be transferred from one position to another is essential in today's workplace. Fine-tuning your computer

> *The future belongs to those who see possibilities before they become obvious. When you see the bandwagon coming down the road, it is too late.*
>
> —Unknown

Shutterstock

Can you multitask without getting too distracted and accomplishing nothing?

Are you sure you are not posting photos that can come back to haunt you?

skills can set you apart from many of today's applicants. Your skills should include the ability to work with word-processing programs, spreadsheets, databases, and PowerPoint. Some careers will require knowledge and expertise of industry software, and you will need to be an expert if this is true in your field. Learn to develop webpages, and create your own website that reflects a professional, career-oriented person. Learn to use social media for more than socializing.

CONTINUE TO GET EXPERIENCE AND EDUCATION. Never stop learning! You may not want to hear it, but your education will never end. Your formal schooling will eventually come to an end, but as long as you are working in today's global economy, you will need to keep abreast of the changes in your field. Seek out opportunities to expand your knowledge base. Get certified in areas that will make you more marketable. Take a continuing education course to brush up on changing workplace skills. Earn an advanced degree. Make yourself the best, most knowledgeable, well-rounded applicant in the field.

AVOID INTERNET AND SOCIAL MEDIA BLUNDERS. Don't let social media mistakes come back to haunt you and cause you to miss out on your dream job! You may think that posting that photo of yourself half-naked with a bottle of bourbon in one hand and a stuffed poodle in the other is cute and that your friends will love it. They may. Your current or future employer may not. Whether you like it or not, employers don't want people who do not represent them well. What you post online today may very well come back to haunt you in the future—even if you remove it, it can still be accessed. You may not lose your current position over a crazy, spur-of-the-moment posting, but it could cost you a future position. You may tell yourself that your Facebook, LinkedIn, or webpage is private and no one's business, but remember, nothing is private online, and everything is someone's business in the world of business.

Would your credit rating help or hurt your career? What can you do to improve it?

WATCH YOUR CREDIT RATING. Building a good credit rating is one of the most important jobs you have. "Really?" you may think. "My credit rating? What in the world does my credit score have to do with my employment?" The answer: A great deal. More and more, employers are accessing your credit history and score as a part of the hiring procedure. Why? Because some employers believe that your credit history paints a clear picture of your working future. Bad credit history means a bad employee. Missed payments mean missed work. Low score means low morale. Careless errors mean a careless job performance. This is just one of the many ways that your credit history and score can follow you for years.

You want to be the most educated, the most brilliant, the most exciting, the most versatile, the most creative individual in the world because then, you can give it away. The only reason you have anything is to give it away.

—Leo Buscaglia, Ph.D.

REMAIN OPEN-MINDED. The ability to accept, appreciate, and interact with a highly diverse workplace and the inherent differences and cultures that will be commonplace is important. You will need to develop the ability to listen to others with whom you disagree or with whom you may have little in common and learn from them and their experiences. The ability to learn a new language (even if your mastery is only at a primitive, broken, conversational level) and the ability to conduct yourself in a respectable and professional style will set you apart from other employees.

PRACTICE ACCOUNTABILITY. The ability to accept responsibility and be accountable for all aspects of your future—including your psychological and spiritual well being, your relationships, your health, your finances, and your overall survival skills—is vitally important. Basically, you must develop a plan for the future that states, "If this fails, I'll do this," or "If this job is phased out, I'll do this," or "If this resource is gone, I'll use this," or "If this person won't help me, this one will."

POLISH YOUR HUMAN RELATIONS SKILLS. Polish your people skills and learn to get along with people from all walks of life. We saved this one for last, certainly not because it is least important, but because this quality is an overriding characteristic of everything listed previously. Employers are looking for individuals who have "people skills." This concept goes so much further than being a team player; it goes to the heart of many workplaces. It touches on your most basic nature, and it draws from your most inner self. The ability to get along with grouchy, cranky, mean, disagreeable, burned-out coworkers is, indeed, a rare quality. But don't be mistaken: There are those who do this, and do it well. Peak performers, or those at the "top of their game," have learned that this world is made up of many types of people, and there is never going to be a time when one of those cranky, grumpy people is not in our midst. Smile. Be nice. Remain positive.

Take some time now and work through the exercise in Figure 5.4. You will find several skills and traits for which employers are looking in the left-hand column. In the right-hand column, create two tips that outline ways *you* can impress an employer.

MOVING UP THE LADDER

How Do I Get Promoted?

When you start to work, you should make every effort to do an outstanding job in your current position, but you should also start thinking about how you are going to get promoted to your next position. You might even need to make a lateral move that better positions you to move up, so don't rule out such an offer before thinking about it carefully. Does a lateral move better position you in a track that will allow you to move up faster? In addition to the items previously listed, you need to pay attention to these hints:

- Give your employer an honest day's work for an honest day's pay. Don't slack off even if everyone else does. Get to work on time; don't take an extra long lunch; don't take sick leave unless you are sick; don't waste time chatting and gossiping when you should be working; and don't play games and send unprofessional e-mail at work.

- Plan every day in detail. Don't go to work and wander around in the desert. Hit the ground running. Do the big, important jobs that will get you noticed first.

- Be nice to your coworkers. Write thoughtful notes; send birthday cards; bring snacks; and use your manners.

- Try to get a mentor who can provide guidance for you. Mentors can spread good news about you and help you get noticed for your accomplishments. People above you on the career ladder often know information that will be helpful to you. If someone mentors you, you need to be prepared to return the favor by helping him or her.

- Support your boss! Make the boss look good, and he or she will not forget! Make your boss look bad, and he or she won't forget this either.

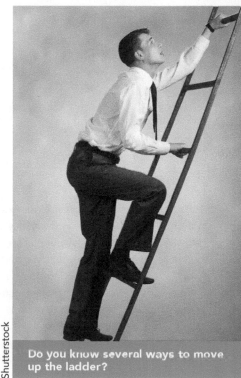

Shutterstock

Do you know several ways to move up the ladder?

Figure 5.4 Skills for Gainful Employment

Skill/Trait Employers Seek	Two Tips To Impress
Priority/Time management	1.
	2.
Attitude	1.
	2.
Written communication	1.
	2.
Interpersonal communication/Relationships	1.
	2.
Ethics	1.
	2.
Dress/Personal grooming	1.
	2.
Computer/Technology skills	1.
	2.
Decision-making / Problem-solving skills	1.
	2.
Confidence	1.
	2.
Advanced training/Certifications	1.
	2.

POSITIVE HABITS at Work

Plan to be successful by developing a career plan. Work on your plan every day by observing what successful people are doing. Adjust your plan when you find a better way of doing things. Pay the price to be successful by going back to school, taking in-house seminars, or learning a language. Build good relationships with internal and external customers. Include in your plan the ability to survive and thrive if you are outsourced.

When you have a formal evaluation, let your boss know that you want to move up and seek his or her advice as to what you need to do to be successful.

- Sell yourself. Send reports to your boss detailing your accomplishments. Do this in a modest way, but be sure your boss knows what you are doing. There is an old saying that is very true: "He who tooteth not his own horn, the same shall not be tooted."

- Build a network inside and outside the company. The more people you know, the better. Take advantage of any opportunity to make good connections. Join professional organizations, volunteer for jobs, and go to lunch with different people in a variety of positions and companies. The next promotion you get may be in an entirely different company.

- Stand out from the pack. Come early; stay late. Go the extra mile. Dress sharp, regardless of what everyone else is doing. Help other people when they are swamped, as long as you have done your work. Never say, "That's not in my job description." Have something worthwhile to say in meetings—do your homework!

- Take solutions to your boss. Bosses get problems reported to them and dumped on their desks every day. It's fine to tell your boss there's a problem. It's great to be able to say, "Here's how to solve it."

- Be willing to move! Some people are willing to go anywhere. They'll jump at the chance to go work in India or China, whereas others don't want to leave their hometown. If you are willing to move—at least for the first few years—your chances of moving up faster are increased.

CREATING MULTIPLE REVENUE STREAMS

How Can I Earn and Save Money in Addition to My Salary?

Smart people learn early the value of multiple sources of income. There are many reasons to earn extra money: First, you can save it or invest it; second, you can develop new skills that might lead to your own business; and third, this income can tide you over if you lose your main source of income. Because of today's volatile job market, we highly encourage you to develop at least one alternate source of income. "How do I do this?" you might ask. Be creative. What are your talents and skills? Who can you partner with to start a part-time business? Some suggestions follow (though this is by no means a complete list):

- Are you musically talented? Can you play in a band? Can you perform children's music at parties? Can you be a disk jockey? Can you be a pianist for a small church that needs a part-time musician?

- Can you paint houses on the weekends?

- Can you have a booth at craft shows and sell materials?

- Can you make jewelry and sell it on the Internet?

- Can you buy and sell things on eBay?

- Can you design websites or perform other computing services for small companies?

- Are you good with accounting? Could you keep books and file reports for small companies?

- Are you good with children? Can you babysit on the weekends? Can you start a service using reliable friends?

- Are you good with landscaping? Could you and a friend start a part-time landscaping business?

- Are you especially talented in an academic subject? Can you provide tutoring for a high school or middle school student? Can you start a service business? Can you work for an established tutoring service?

Shutterstock

What skills do you have that you could turn into additional revenue streams?

The list of creative ideas is endless. The point is: Get started now! If and when you really need this money to survive, you will have saved enough to pay your bills, and you will still have income. If the worst-case scenario never happens, you can take a great vacation to China or Africa or buy a house or work on a master's degree. Use your talents to build security and confidence.

DOWNSIZING, RIGHTSIZING, RIFS, TERMINATIONS, OUTSOURCING, LAYOFFS

How Would I Survive Losing My Job?

> Barn's burnt down . . .
> now I can see the moon.
> —Masahide, Japanese philosopher
> (1657–1723)

Today it is quite common for employees to get the dreaded "pink slip" (letter telling an employee that they have been let go from their job) when they have done nothing to deserve it. If this happens to you, you should know that it is normal to be scared, disoriented, and depressed, but it is not the end of the world. You can overcome it and perhaps even do better.

In a tight economy, many companies find that they have too many employees to support relative to the income they are producing, so they have to reduce their workforce. If this happens to you, you need to be prepared. There are lots of qualified people looking for work, so you have to be focused and strategic when finding your next employment. Hopefully, you have initiated another source of income and can survive a few months while you search for the right job. You should always keep your resumé updated and ready to use at a minute's notice.

Try not to become adrift and depressed; instead, look at this event as an opportunity to do something totally new that might be a better fit for you. Sometimes it takes something like losing a job to force us out of our comfort zone and help us realize our potential. This may be the perfect time to reinvent yourself as the person you always wished you could be.

Being prepared for loss of job includes the following steps:

- Sign up for unemployment benefits the same day you lose your job. There is a period of about three weeks before you will start receiving benefits.
- Before you leave your job, copy all e-mail addresses, phone numbers, and contacts.
- If you have a company cell phone, copy the information to your own phone.
- Get your own personal e-mail address if you don't have one so employers can reach you and so you can file resumés online.
- Protect your credit rating. Try to make your minimum payments, but let your creditors know if you are having problems.
- Put your resumé on LinkedIn, Monster.com, Careerbuilder, and TheLadders.
- Look up the term "resumé blasting" and follow the directions for this process.
- Don't burn any bridges with the employer who laid you off. Your next job may be a recall from that company.
- Mobilize yourself. Quit moping about your bad luck, get off the couch, and mix and mingle with people who might have leads for jobs. Let your friends and colleagues know that you are looking for a job, and provide them with your resumé.
- If you have joined professional organizations, let the people you know in these groups that you are searching for a job.
- Attend career fairs and employment agencies that might be able to help you find work.

- Go to the gym. Exercise will produce chemicals that are a natural high, and it takes stress out of your body. If you feel better, you are likely to "sell" better to people looking for employees. Protect your health during this stressful time.

- Consider temporary employment that can help you pay the bills.

- If you have children, keep them at home temporarily instead of using expensive day care.

- Cut your grocery bills by eating less expensively.

- Rent movies instead of going to the theater.

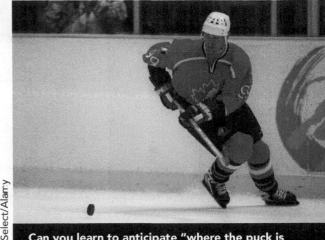

Can you learn to anticipate "where the puck is going" when it relates to your future?

As you can see, there are strategies to follow to avoid outsourcing or to survive it and thrive when it happens to you. You might want to consider this tip: "Go where the puck is going!" Sound crazy? The great hockey champ Wayne Gretzky made the comment that this one step had been his key to success. What does it mean? He said that when he was playing hockey, he did not skate to where the puck was at the moment—he skated to where the puck was going. He anticipated the direction of where the puck was going to be hit, and when it came his way, he was already there—ready to play.

Think of your career in this light. Go to companies that will be bright in the future, not necessarily where it is bright at this moment. Look ahead and try to determine what is going to be "hot" in the coming years, not what is hot right now. Plan ahead. Look at trends. Read. Ask questions. Stay prepared. Try to work in *sunrise industries* (those businesses that are new and emerging, such as solar energy), not *sunset industries* (textile factories). Think in the future tense, not the present.

DESIGNING A CAREER PLAN

What Steps Do I Need to Take to Chart My Course?

This is not an easy, one-hour assignment. It takes time to think through your entire career and to design a plan that will take you where you aspire to go. You should know that this plan will change as you move up the ladder and as your confidence, skills, and knowledge grow. There is no doubt, however, that you will be far better off with a plan than you are just drifting along hoping someone will notice you and give you a promotion. A career plan will focus your efforts on doing all the right things to be successful. Simply looking at the next job down the road is not designing a career plan!

Before you chart your career path, you need to take an introspective look by considering the questions in Figure 5.5. You need to know what brings you happiness before you move toward the wrong career. After you have studied Figure 5.5, begin developing your own career plan. Don't be concerned if you can't complete the plan right now; the important thing is to start and continue.

Now you are ready to begin charting your path. Remember, this may take months, even years, because it will change as you move forward. The important thing is to always have a career plan. The great majority of people will not have a career plan; this plan puts you way ahead of the competition because you know what you want and have determined what you must do to get it. Study the sample career plan in Figure 5.6.

Rings and gems are not gifts. They are only imitations of gifts. The only true gift one can give is himself.
—Unknown

Figure 5.5 A Career Plan

1. What kind of work do you want to do? _____
   _____

2. What are you passionate about? _____
   _____

3. Are you a people person? Why or why not? _____
   _____

4. Do you want to live in a large city? _____
   _____

5. Are you willing to move around? Would you like a job that leads to an international position? _____
   _____

6. What are your strongest values? Does the company you are interested in match your values? _____
   _____

7. What kind of organization best fits your needs? Do you need to work for a large company or a small company, or do you
   need to start your own business? _____
   _____

8. Can you deal with the stress of a high-powered career, or would you be happier in a more laid-back type of work?
   _____
   _____

9. Are your career aspirations really yours, or are you trying to please someone else? _____
   _____

10. Are you driven by money or a feeling of satisfaction in doing a good job and in doing what you always wanted to do?
   _____
   _____

Now, answer two more questions before you begin designing your career plan.

What does "happiness" mean to you? (What would it look like? How would it feel? What would you be doing? What
would you have? Who would you be with? How do you spend your leisure time? Do you have a family?)

What is "success" for you? (What does it look like? What are you doing? Who are you working for or with? How much money
are you making? How does it feel? What are the rewards of success?)

Figure 5.6 Model Career Plan

What I Want to Achieve:

Having majored in business, I want to find an entry-level position that offers upward mobility according to how hard I work and how I use my education and abilities. I would like to begin my career as a consultant with a major consulting firm that will expose me to a variety of aspects of business and provide an entry into a company that matches my goals and aspirations. From that position, I would like to move into management, begin my MBA in international business, learn to speak Mandarin, and move to my dream company, XYZ, where I hope to attain a management position that will lead me to an executive management position.

Job 1: Business consultant

Skills required: Degree in business administration; in-house training with company, working with a team to learn the consulting area; excellent soft skills; specific technology and software skills; report-writing skills.

Skills assessment: I have degree, excellent soft skills, need more training on software, need to improve report-writing skills.

Duties and responsibilities: I will be working with a team to recommend IT practices, accounting systems, and interviewing skills.

Plan to get this job: Take a course in report writing, teach myself accounting software, send resumés to top 10 companies for business consulting, network with people I know who are doing this kind of work.

[After getting his first consulting position, Josh should then begin preparing to become a manager. He needs to pay attention to other managers, as well as his own. He needs to let HR and his supervisor know that he would like to move toward a supervisor position and would like to take advantage of any special training.]

Job 2: Supervisor of business consultants

Skills required: Ability to lead and manage other people, ability to delegate, ability to shape a vision for a group; skills in evaluation, excellent soft skills, sales ability.

Skills assessment: I need to take seminars in leading and managing and salesmanship; need to study visionary planning, how to evaluate people.

Duties and responsibilities: I will be leading a team of consultants and evaluating their performance; I will have

to sell our team to businesses as consultants; I will have to be able to delegate and make decisions.

Plan to get this job: Do an excellent job as a consultant; let management know I want to be a supervisor, take advantage of any in-house training available; take courses at the community college; build excellent relationships with people internally and externally; begin working on MBA in international business at night and on weekends; taking a course in Mandarin at community college; spend vacation in China.

[Assume Josh has done well in the first two jobs and he is now ready to seek employment in management with another company. You cannot plan to stay with the same company for your entire career; that rarely happens today. Remember, "go where the puck is going." XYZ is an international company that can ultimately offer Josh the opportunity to work in China, which is one of his top career goals. Do you see how Josh's plan is building on each previous position and how he will ultimately reach his top goal?]

Job #3: Sales position in XYZ Company

Skills required: Degree in business administration; Mandarin is an asset; international travel is considered a plus; sales and management experience required; ability to build relationships with clients; ability to learn XYZ software and technology.

Skills assessment: Have degree and working on MBA; learning Mandarin; have been to China; have sales and management experience; have built excellent relationships with external clients and could get recommendations from them; have ability to learn the software and technology based on past experience.

Duties and responsibilities: I will be a member of a team that sells XYZ software to international companies; some international travel required; ability to interact with international customers; must demonstrate software and technology and be able to make excellent presentations.

Plan to get this job: Send resumé with recommendations from several external clients; ask Mr. Robinson, who works at XYZ, to put in a good word for me; have my Mandarin professor write a letter about how well I am doing in this class; emphasize my international travel experience and desire to travel internationally; emphasize that I have almost completed MBA in international business.

[Notice how Josh is anticipating what is required for his next career move. He is not "letting things happen"; he

(continued)

Figure 5.6 Model Career Plan (continued)

is making things happen. He has prepared to be successful by anticipating what skills and knowledge are required and gradually accumulating all of them. Success does not just happen. Success is planned!]

Job 4: Manager of international sales team in XYZ Company

Skills required: Master's degree in business administration; experience in a variety of business areas including accounting and IT; knowledge of software and technology; ability to shape a vision for a department; ability to lead a team and to build external relationships with customers; fluent Mandarin or Spanish skills; excellent salesmanship abilities.

Skills assessment: Lack one course in MBA program; program included Advanced Salesmanship and Advanced Communications and Presentation Skills; have experience in leading others and shaping a vision for a team; have excellent relationships with external businesses; need to learn company-specific software for XYZ; learning Mandarin.

Duties and responsibilities: I lead a team that will sell XYZ's exclusive software to international companies; must be able to set priorities for team; shape a vision; interact with international clients; be able to travel internationally; must speak Mandarin; must have excellent communication and presentation skills.

Plan to get this job: Let the management team making the selection know I want this job and tell them what I have been doing to prepare for it; share my portfolio that includes travel to China, Mandarin course, communications and presentation skills, and examples of presentations I have made; try to get my manager to recommend me.

[If Josh gets this job and continues to prepare as he has been doing, he will most likely reach his goal of being a member of the Executive Team at XYZ. His career opportunities and desires may change along the way, but regardless, he has set himself up to be successful because he had a plan, he worked hard and smart, and he went where the puck was going.]

Reflections: PUTTING IT ALL TOGETHER

After reading this chapter, you have realized that change will be an important part of your life and career, and how you deal with it will no doubt have a big impact on your success. We encourage you to embrace change, anticipate changes that are coming down the road, and plan for change. It is very important for you to develop a career plan that will guide you and help you realize your ambitions much faster. We hope you will also prepare for a potential loss of employment at some time during your career by using multiple sources of revenue to cushion the blow, as well as provide more income for investments, savings, and entertainment.

DIGITAL BRIEFCASE

CONNECTING WITH BUSINESS COLLEAGUES THROUGH LINKEDIN

LinkedIn is a professional network designed to help businesspeople interact. Think of it as Facebook for business. It is a great tool for increasing visibility and can assist you in showcasing your expertise. When beginning your job search, a great place to start is by creating a profile on

LinkedIn and then making connections with people you know. You can use LinkedIn to connect with current and former colleagues, supervisors, and clients.

Use the following tips to get started in creating and using your LinkedIn profile.

- Before you begin, think about what your want to accomplish with your LinkedIn profile. Do you want to expand your network, are you looking for a job, or are you looking to reconnect with colleagues from former jobs who may be able to recommend you?

- First, follow the steps to register on the LinkedIn.com site.

- Click on the "Profile" link.

- Click on "Edit Contact Settings" and choose the types of people with whom you want to connect.

- Click "Save Changes."

- Next, select an attractive, professional headshot.

- Post a profile summary that is honest and discusses results of things you have accomplished that might interest an employer. Keep it simple and straightforward and not too long. You can list your education, honors, and awards in other sections of your profile, but your summary should be brief and to the point.

- For *each company you have worked for*, fill in the job title and describe your duties. You can click on the link right below the position field, which can provide you assistance in describing your duties.

- When you have finished listing your positions, you can enter information about your education into your profile. You will see that LinkedIn provides a pull-down menu that allows you to search for your institution. You can add information about your degree, your major, the date your attended the school, and other information about your educational experience.

- Work experience and education are the two main parts of your profile, but if you scroll down, you will see places where you can add information such as your website, interests, awards, and other items.

- Once you have completed your profile, read it one more time to check for errors and to be sure that it represents you in an exemplary manner. You can always go back and change or add things later.

- Click the tab "View My Profile" at the top of the profile screen to see how others will see your profile.

- Finally, look over to the right and locate a link that says "Edit Public Profile Settings" and select "Full View." Then you can choose the features that you want to be visible to anyone who accesses your profile.

- Finally, if you are happy with your profile, click "Save Changes" down at the bottom of the screen.

REFERENCES

Association of American Colleges and Universities. (2007). *College learning for the new global century.* Retrieved June 28, 2011, from www.aacu.org/leap/documents/GlobalCentury_final.pdf.

ASVAB. (2009). Career exploration program. Retrieved June 23, 2011, from www.asvab program.com/downloads/ASVABIdeaSkillsMostValued.pdf.

Eby, L. T., Casper, W. J., Lockwood, A., Bordeaux, C., & Brinley, A. (2005). *Work interference with life domains.* Retrieved July 29, 2011, from www.shrm.org/about/foundation/research/Documents/Ryan%20Final%20Report%20610.pdf

Life-Work Balance
The Marnie Pearce Professionalism Program

1. Identify personal characteristics to effectively interact with internal and external environments.

5. Identify potential questions and concerns for future interview situations.

7. Identify and research current trends in the workplace

8. Investigate resources to assist in professional development.

How can you begin to find JOY in work?

How can you begin to find JOY in leisure?

(24 Hour Day)

Ideal Life Chart

Self Community Spiritual	Money Career Health Relations

Current Life Chart

Self Community Spiritual	Money Career Health Relations

Printed Name_____

119

PART THREE:
MANAGING YOUR CAREER

chapter six

CONNECT

CREATING AND MAINTAINING A PROFESSIONAL NETWORK

Never before in history has innovation offered so much promise to so many in such a short time.
—Bill Gates, Microsoft founder

PART THREE: MANAGING YOUR CAREER

PROFESSIONALISM DEFINED

How Do I Become a Professional?

Professionalism is defined by a number of characteristics and traits: your character, which is who you are; your knowledge which is what you know and what experiences you can draw on; and your image which is how you project yourself and how others perceive you. A true professional cares deeply about what the job is and how well it is done, and, at the same time, cares about the company for which he or she works and the colleagues with whom they work. Professionals are willing to go above and beyond to be sure that customers and colleagues are taken care of in an exemplary manner.

SETTING YOURSELF APART AND FINDING YOUR DIRECTION

How Do You Separate Yourself from the Pack?

How do you distinguish yourself from the countless job seekers out there? What are you going to do that sets you apart from your competition? What do you have to offer that no one else can possibly offer to an employer? What unique skills do you have to help you thrive and survive in a rapidly changing world where outsourcing is commonplace and technology is constantly evolving? Answering these questions is the primary focus of this chapter, and indeed, this book and the course in which you are presently enrolled.

You laugh at me because I am different. I laugh at you because you are all the same.

—Unknown

In his book *The 2010 Meltdown,* Edward Gordon (2008) writes, "Simply stated, today in America, there are just too many people trained for the wrong jobs. Many jobs have become unnecessary, technically obsolete . . . or worse yet, the job/career aspirations of too many current and future workers are at serious odds with the changing needs of the U.S. labor market." An example of this disconnect between the workforce and the market place can be found in this fact: **Eight million U.S. workers speak English so poorly that they cannot hold high-paying jobs** (Center for Law and Social Policy). Conversely, people who are highly skilled, possess superb oral and written communication skills, know how to solve problems, have excellent technology skills, and can work well with others should be in great demand for many years to come.

Careers in the following areas are projected for high growth in the coming decade: **health sciences** (dental assistants, home health aids, physician assistants, medical assistants, occupational therapy, physical therapist, cardiovascular technologists, etc.), **aviation** (airplane mechanics and air traffic controllers), **skilled trades** (plumbers, electricians, mechanics, etc.); **teaching** (K–12 and college); **technology** (aerospace and GPS engineers, water and sanitation engineers, transportation services, systems analyst, programmers, interactive media designers, software engineers, desktop publishing, database administrators, etc.), and **management, marketing, and public relations** (business managers, human resource directors, advertising and public relations, accounting, etc.).

Figure 6.1   How to Work a Room Like a Pro

- Survey the room before you enter to get "the lay of the land."

- If you have a drink, hold it in your left hand so your right hand is free to shake hands. Don't have more than one drink!

- Avoid eating. It is difficult to talk, eat, balance a plate, and shake hands. Eat before you go! You are there to do business, not eat. The worst thing you can do is to load up your plate and act like this is your last meal.

- Don't cluster in the corner with the only person you know! Move around the room, shaking hands and introducing yourself. Take the initiative. Most people will be glad you did.

- Focus on the other person. Smile and be friendly. Talk for a few minutes and move on.

- Sell yourself with a sound bite—something interesting about yourself. For example: "I'm John Martin, the new admissions coordinator at Marion Hospital."

- Don't look around the room or over the other person's shoulder while you're talking to someone. Look at the person as though he or she is the most interesting person in the room. Use the person's name.

- Don't talk about politics, make fun of a state, or tell religious or ethnic jokes. You never know whom you might offend.

- Don't talk about your health. People find this very boring. No one wants to hear about your operation or extensive details about your vacation.

- Converse a few minutes, excuse yourself, and move on. The idea is to meet people and network.

How to Work a Room

As a businessperson, you probably will attend cocktail parties. You should consider them an extension of work. You are there to make contacts, make a good impression, network, expand your client base, and generally represent your company in a positive manner. In other words, you should work the room. Consider the basic tips in Figure 6.1 for working a room.

Business parties, receptions, and cocktail parties should be treated as an extension of work. You should look your best, present yourself well, and consider these events as a great opportunity to network.

NETWORKING

How Do I Form a Circle of Peers in the World of Work?

It will be important for you to develop a network among the people you know who may work for a company in which you have an interest. People on the inside have an advantage in helping you get your foot in the door. What about your dad's coworker? Your wife's friend? What about a friend who knows your work style and works for a company in which you have an interest? Use every legal, moral, and ethical method you have to get the interview. Some important networking opportunities include:

- Attending events and conferences on and off campus
- Joining professional organizations in your field of study
- Shadowing professionals in your field
- Volunteering within your community
- Working in externships or internships in your field
- Contacting family and friends about opportunities
- Logging onto websites and job search sites such as:

  - www.monster.com
  - www.career.com
  - www.careerbuilder.com
  - www.indeed.com
  - www.craigslist.com

- Talking to your instructors
- Working with headhunters or recruiters
- Contacting a temp agency in the city in which you hope to work
- Working with your school's counselors and career officers

HRSM Alumni Society Career Night
The Marnie Pearce Professionalism Program

Background: Going to an event with the intention of making new contacts can be intimidating for college graduates and those unaccustomed to building professional relationships. The invited alumni and friends of the College of HRSM are here to not only connect with our graduates, but to help **YOU** practice the art of conversation.

Course Objectives: This event is meant to be a practice in "face-to-face" communication. The career night is designed to assist students in cultivating a positive professional image while enhancing your social business skills via mock performance in a realistic setting.

Program: The Alumni Society Career Night is designed as a professional cocktail reception. Everyone will receive a nametag and program upon entering. Light refreshments will be available throughout the evening with no formal agenda. In order to keep the student to networker ratio low, there will be three rounds of networking.

Role of the Student: You are to practice the skill of "Working a Room" by joining conversations, introducing yourself, and making meaningful professional dialogue. Do not become a "wall flower" or monopolize one Alumni/Networker. Have a meaningful interaction with as many as you can in the allotted time. You will be given 3-4 feedback cards to hand over to a networker so that they may provide you with personal feedback. **They will be evaluating your professional appearance, conversation and employability.**

Role of the Alumni/Networker: The Alumni/Networkers will be well-informed that the objective is to give HRSM students an opportunity to practice networking. They will need to take some responsibility for facilitating conversations and exemplifying social skills and effective networking interactions. They may have business cards to pass along to those students who succeed in making a meaningful connection. Some opportunity will be available for the Alumni/Networkers to also connect. There are no obligations or expectations to conduct interviews or hire our students. Follow-up with students is certainly encouraged.

In-Class Follow-up: Instructors will spend some class time discussing the experience. The students will report back in some manner or answer questions such as: What went well for you? What was most difficult? What are you doing now to build your professional network? As part of the Practical Exam, each student will verify their strength in this area.

Student Name: _____

129

chapter seven

PLAN

CREATING A DYNAMIC EMPLOYMENT PACKAGE AND JOB SEARCH PLAN

No one can tell you what your life's work is,

but it is important that you find it. There is a part

of you that already knows; affirm that part.

—Willis W. Harman

OVERVIEW OF THE HUMAN RESOURCES DEPARTMENT

How Do They Manage All These Requirements?

Human resource management (HRM) is engaging people (employees) in a variety of ways and at different levels to accomplish an organization's goals and objectives. Human resource managers and employees work on a diverse array of responsibilities, ranging from recruiting to staffing to training to compensating to evaluating employees. This department is in charge of annual leave and vacations, sick leave, discrimination policies, social security deductions, taxes, retirement funds, and employee privacy. In addition, they must comply with government laws and rules such as safety regulations, and they must oversee internal corporate policies and procedures. At times, HR professionals must deal with unions and labor relations and negotiations. The illustration in Figure 7.1 shows the major functions in the HR process.

"In a large corporation, the *director of human resources* may supervise several departments, each headed by an experienced manager who most likely specializes in one human resources

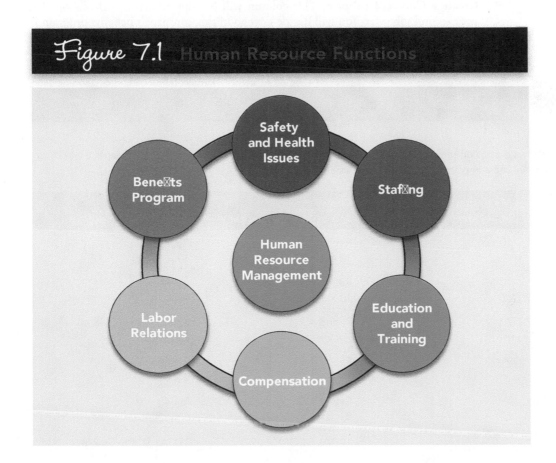

Figure 7.1 Human Resource Functions

activity, such as employment and placement, compensation and benefits, training and development, or labor relations. The director may report to a top human resources executive" (U.S. Department of Labor, 2010–2011). In small companies, the HR department may consist of a manager and a few employees with multiple responsibilities.

MAKING AN IMPORTANT CHOICE

How Do I Decide Which Job to Accept?

One of the most effective ways to make a decision is to use a numerical scale to actually assign a "grade" to each choice before you. This exercise is designed to help you make a choice between two job offers in relation to benefits. Of course, benefits are not the only major factor you have to consider when choosing between two jobs, but it is one of the most important components. This decision chart works in the following way:

- **Create an Element (benefit) column.** This column lists the aspects of the decision that are important to you, such as pay, potential for growth, joy of work, and so on.
- **Create a Rating of Importance column.** This column gives each element a rating that *you* assign. Using a scale of 1 to 10, you will decide if a particular benefit is very important (an 8, 9, or 10) or if it is not very important (a 1, 2, or 3).
- **Create a Choice 1 column.** This column will list the numerical calculations for your first job offer. You will decide how good this company's benefits program is in terms of a specific benefit and then multiply that number by your importance rating.
- **Create a Choice 2 column.** This column will list the numerical calculations for your second job offer. You will decide how good this company's benefits program is in terms of a specific benefit and then multiply that number by your importance rating. Once you have created your columns (see Figure 7.2), you will work through

Figure 7.2 Samantha's Decision-Making Chart

The following example shows a decision-making chart between two job offers for Samantha. The Element (benefit) column lists the items that are most important to Samantha in selecting a new job.

Element (benefit)	My Rating of Importance 1–10	Choice 1 Job at Mercy Hospital	Choice 2 Job at Grace Hospital
Health insurance	10	Rating = 5 $10 \times 5 = 50$	Rating = 8 $10 \times 8 = 80$
Child care	10	Rating = 9 $10 \times 9 = 90$	Rating = 7 $10 \times 7 = 70$
Flexible schedule	7	Rating = 2 $7 \times 2 = 14$	Rating = 5 $7 \times 5 = 35$
Retirement plan	9	Rating = 9 $9 \times 9 = 81$	Rating = 5 $9 \times 5 = 45$
Paid vacation	8	Rating = 8 $8 \times 8 = 64$	Rating = 6 $8 \times 6 = 48$
		TOTAL SCORE = 299	TOTAL SCORE = 278

Figure 7.3 Decision-Making Chart

Element (benefit)	My Rating of Importance 1–10	Choice 1	Choice 2
		TOTAL SCORE =	**TOTAL SCORE =**

your decisions using your head and your heart. Assume Samantha has been offered two jobs. Review how she rated each benefit for the two different companies to help her make a decision about which job to accept.

As you can see, Samantha's best option in terms of benefits is Mercy Hospital. A numerical score may not be the ultimate way to make a decision, but at least you have taken the time to think about what is important to you, what is offered within the choices, and how it ranks in importance to you. By using this system, you are calling on your head and your heart to make decisions that could affect your life for a very long time.

Now, using the top five benefits that you selected above, insert them into the Decision-Making Chart in Figure 7.3. For purposes of this exercise, you can make up information about the two jobs.

BIGGEST INTERVIEW *Blunders*

Quan landed an interview with a company that was seeking a person for her dream job. She prepared carefully, dressed well, and arrived on time. But only a few minutes into the interview, Quan interrupted the interviewer to ask about benefits, telling the interviewer, "Benefits are my main consideration in accepting a position." Quan should have waited until the second interview to bring up benefits, or she should have given the interviewer time to introduce the subject during the interview. Because Quan appeared to be much more interested in her own compensation than she was in doing a good job for the company, she did not get the job.

LESSON: Wait until the second interview to mention salary and benefits. The interviewer knows you are interested and will most likely discuss it with you before you have to ask.

PLANNING FOR THE FUTURE

What Am I Going to Do for the Rest of My Life?

"What am I going to do for the rest of my life?" is an overwhelming question for anyone, especially in a dramatically changing, global, technologically driven environment. What was true last year—and sometimes even last week—is no longer true. While many things that worked for your parents and grandparents are still important and relevant today—like ethics, integrity, hard work, education, honesty, teamwork—many practices that were true in their time are no longer valid. Your grandfather may have gone to work for a company and stayed there all his life. Employers were loyal to employees, and employees were loyal to the company. Work stayed pretty much the same one year to the next. All that has changed. You will have many different jobs during your lifetime—you will most likely have at least three or four different careers, and what constitutes your work will be constantly changing.

What changes do you foresee coming in your chosen career field in the next five years?

iStockPhoto

Getting a job, the *right job*, is hard work. Many people in the career development field would say that finding the right job is a full-time job. We agree. One thing that you should have in mind as you begin your job search is that this process is not easy and it is totally yours. No one can complete your job search plan, application packet, and interview but you. Sure, people from your institution's career planning office will help you, but ultimately, you are on your own.

> *The four great questions: Why are you here? Where have you been? Where are you going? What difference will you make?*
>
> —Hal Simon

You will need to use every tool in your toolbox to find the job for which you've prepared. You will need to call on the career services office at your institution, scour the Internet for job postings—including corporate websites—use all of your personal and social networking contacts, quiz your instructors about possible leads, read the want-ads, post your resumé with an online job bank or a site such as Monster or LinkedIn, attend job fairs, and possibly even contact an employment or "headhunter" agency. In today's crazy, upside-down job market, you'll need to do everything you can to get your foot in the door. This chapter will help you create an outstanding impression through your cover letter, resumé, reference choices, and business cards so that you can do just that.

Your Positive Attitude and the Job Search

Today is the day that I am going to find my dream job. Today is the day that I am going to put my talents, knowledge, and experience to use. Today is the day that I will get to show people just what I can do. Today is the day that I am going to start my professional career.

Today is just another horrible day without a job, and it ain't never going to get any better. Today is another report about high unemployment. Today is the day when more jobs are being shipped abroad. Today is the day I stay home, watch *I Love Lucy* , and just try to forget that I paid all this money for a degree I can't use.

Do you see the difference between these two people? Granted, a positive attitude is not the only thing that you need as you begin your job search, but it is certainly important. Will you hit walls during your search? Yes. Will you meet with rejection? Yes. Will you be frustrated? Yes. These things happen in the best of times. They most certainly are happening now. However, when you have a positive attitude about your search and what you have to offer, this comes across to the people who will be hiring you. Conversely, your negative attitude will also show. You may not notice it, but your attitude affects your actions, speech, interview responses, and nonverbal communication. Choose to be positive.

Career Objective

As you begin your job search both mentally and in writing, the place to begin is with a career objective. A career objective is an introductory statement written for your resumé. It is the only place on your resumé where you can use the words *I, me,* or *my.* This is a personal statement that briefly (usually one sentence) describes your desires, talents, skills, and interest in a specific position. Your career objective will not only make your resumé stronger, it also forces you to prepare mentally for what you really have to offer and what you want in a career.

Think of your career objective as *"an elevator speech."* Pretend you are on an elevator with your dream employer. You have the time span of two floors to tell Mr. Jamison about yourself, your skills, and what you want. Period. Wham! Two floors. What would you say? You need to be able to answer this question before you begin searching for a position, writing a cover letter, or preparing your resumé.

Two career objectives are shown below:

Weak Objective
I want to work as a marketing manager with a major corporation.

Strong Objective
Seeking a marketing position that will utilize my organization talents, oral communication skills, and expertise with Word, Excel, PowerPoint, Prezi, and Facebook in a competitive, engaging, and high-energy environment.

WORKIN' 9 TO 5—OR TRYING TO

Is It Really Possible to Sell Yourself Through a Cover Letter and Resumé?

You've got it all together—education, experience, and a strong sense of self. A positive attitude. What do you do now? How do you pull all of this together? How do you find the job of your dreams? The job for which you have prepared?

Know this! Getting a job—the *right job*—is hard work! Regardless of your status in school, now is the time to begin your job search. If you are in the last months of your program, your job search should be a top priority. If you are just beginning your educational plan, it is never too early to begin assembling a dynamic employment package.

Selling Yourself

Remember the old saying, "You are what you eat"? When searching for a professional position, you could change that to read, "You are what you write." Most likely, the people conducting

What is your elevator speech?

the job search have never met you and know nothing about you except what you provide to them. A carefully crafted resumé communicates your past history (skills and experience) that makes you the ideal candidate for their position. Your resumé is the first marketing piece and in many cases must stand alone when a recruiter is determining whether to interview you. Just as a well-designed and well-written resumé can be a wonderful first step, a poorly designed and written resumé can doom you before you ever leave your house. A good thing to remember is this: A resumé gets you the interview; the interview gets you the job. Although there is no single way to develop your career resumé and formats may vary from discipline to discipline, this chapter will outline the key components of resumés and discuss how to develop a resumé that will represent your best efforts.

Your second "advertising tool" is your cover letter. A cover letter is basically an expansion of your resumé. A cover letter gives you the chance to link your resumé, skills, and experience together with your interest in a specific company's position. You will need to write many cover letters to make this link work properly; in other words, you most likely need to write a cover letter designed for each job for which you apply. Your cover letter will often be the stepping stone to get an employer to even look at your resumé. Consider it "a teaser," if you will, to all of your talents and experience. Just as you would never send someone a greeting card and not sign it, you would never send a resumé and not tell the person or committee why you sent it. Your cover letter tells why.

WRITE A POWERFUL AND CONCISE COVER LETTER

How Do You Get Your Foot in the Door?

Careful preparation must be done **prior to starting** the interview process. Two key elements of this preparation are your cover letter and resumé. Both are key components in your career search.

Whenever you send your resumé to a company, whether it is in response to a posted advertisement or was requested by someone, you must send a cover letter with it. Cover letters are extremely important; in fact, most recruiters say that they read four times as many cover letters as they do resumés because if the cover letter does not "strike a chord," then they never look past it to the resumé.

Career development expert, author, and speaker Carol Robins (2006) states, "During my 25 plus years that I've been involved in career development, I have found that of all the paperwork associated with job searching, cover letters give job searchers the most difficulty." The information presented here will help you overcome any anxiety associated with writing your cover letter or resumé.

As you the process of building your cover letter and resumé, consider the general tips in Figure 7.4.

Simply put, the cover letter's purpose is to get the interviewer to read your resumé. It sets the tone for who you are, what you have to offer, and what you want. "It screams—ever so politely—that you have the intelligence, experience, and soft skills to be the answer to an employer's staffing problem" (Britton-Whitcomb, 2003). The cover letter should say to the reader, "You have an opening and a detailed description of what you need, and I can fill your opening and be the person who gets the job done—and done well."

Consider the following **four steps to success** when writing your cover letter:

Figure 7.4 Tips You Can't Skip to Build an Effective Resumé

- Both your resumé and cover letter *must be typed.* There are no exceptions to this rule. Ever!
- Your cover letter and resumé must be printed on the same type and color of fine-quality paper. Cheap paper sends the message that you don't care. This is not the place or time to pinch pennies; buy excellent quality, 100 percent cotton stock, resumé-quality paper.
- Check your printer and be sure that the print quality is impeccable. Never send a cover letter or resumé with smudges, ink smears, or poor print quality.
- When you print your cover letter and resumé, be certain that the watermark on the paper is turned in the correct direction. Hold it up to the light and you will see the watermark embedded in the paper. This may sound silly and picky, but people notice attention to detail.
- Do not fold your cover letter or resumé. Purchase a packet of 9" × 13" envelopes in which to send your materials.
- Do not handwrite the address on the envelope. Use a label or type the address directly on the envelope. Remember, first impressions are important.
- Never send a generic photocopy of a cover letter or resumé, even on the finest paper.
- Layout, design, font, spacing, and color must be considered in the building of your cover letter and resumé.
- Unless you are specifically asked to do so, never discuss money or salary history in either your cover letter or resumé. This could work against you. When asked for a salary history, use ranges.
- Your resumé and cover letter must be free of errors. That's right, not one single error is acceptable, including grammar, spelling, punctuation, layout/spacing, dates, or content.
- Each cover letter must be signed, preferably in black ink.

1. An effective cover letter will be *personally addressed and job specific.* If at all possible (and yes, it is possible with just a little research), address your letter to a specific person. Avoid at all costs the dreaded "Dear Sir or Madam" or "To Whom It May Concern." In most cases, a phone call to the company will provide the name of the person along with his or her title and address. Always verify spelling, even with common names. This single step can set you apart from lazy job-seekers. Also, make sure you spell the company's name correctly.

2. Once your letter is correctly addressed, your first paragraph should be an "attention grabber" and it should answer the question "Why am I writing?" Susan Britton-Whitcomb, author of *Resumé Magic* (2003), calls this "the carrot." This simply means that your first paragraph should have an interesting fact, an appeal, or maybe even a quote— something that makes the reader (hopefully, your future employer) read further. Your first paragraph should also have a transition statement that makes the reader want to read on. For example, your last statement might read, "With a degree in medical assisting and four years of experience at Desert Medical Center, I know that I can make a valued contribution to Grace Care Center."

3. Your second (and maybe third) paragraph(s) should clearly state why you are qualified for the position you are seeking. Use your cover letter to highlight those areas of your experience that specifically qualify you for the job. Your cover letter is not the time to list all of your qualifications, but to indicate the two or three components that most qualify you for the position and closely match the position announcement. You may also include specific

POSITIVE HABITS *at Work*

After you have found the position for which you have prepared, you need to think into the future and begin planning for your next job search. "What?" you might be saying. "My next job?" Yes! After you begin your new position, you need to create an e-file where you will save information about your successes, acquired skills, and accomplishments so that you can add them to your next resumé. Your resumé is a living document and must be updated extensively each time you apply for a new position. The best way to keep this information organized is to keep an e-file that lists what you have learned from this job. If you learned how to create an Excel spreadsheet, add that to your file. If you sat on a hiring committee, add that to your file. If you were asked to lead a team, add that to your file. Then, when it comes time to update your resumé, you have all of your successes and updated skills in one place.

attributes that may not be on your resumé. The emphasis here is your value. Relate your education, experience, and talents to the company's need. Mention facts and statistics of how you've been successful in the past. Remember, "Employers are not interested in you for your sake, but rather because of what you can bring to the organization. This might sound harsh, but businesspeople have an obligation to improve the success of their organization. If you consistently show how you can help them do this . . . they will be much more motivated to talk to you" (Farr and Kursmark, 2005).

4. Your final paragraph should address the question of "Where do we go from here?" Do not be ambiguous by saying something trite like "I hope to hear from you in the near future," or "If you have any questions please do not hesitate to call me." Remember, your job search is none of the company's business, nor is it their responsibility. Be proactive by stating that you will be following up with a phone call to discuss your resumé and experience(s) in more detail. Make sure that once you have said that you are going to call that you actually do call. Your final paragraph should also continue to express what you can do for the company. You should end your letter with a statement about your qualities and the company's needs, such as "Mr. Thompson, I will call you on Monday, January 24th at 11:30 a.m. to discuss how my past experiences can help streamline operations and continue superior patient care at Grace Care Center."

Don't forget to **sign your letter**.

UNDERSTAND THE DO'S AND DON'TS OF MEMORABLE RESUMÉS

How Do You Sell Yourself?

Eight seconds. That is all you have to gain the attention of your potential employer, according to author and consultant Susan Ireland (2003). "In eight seconds, an employer scans your resumé and decides whether she will invest more time to consider you as a job *candidate*. The secret to passing the eight-second test is to make your resumé look inviting and quick to read" (p. 14).

A resumé is the blueprint that details what you have accomplished with regards to education, experience, skills acquisition, workplace successes, and progressive responsibility and/or leadership. It is a painting (that you are able to "paint") of how your professional life looks. It is the ultimate advertisement of you! Your resumé must create interest and hopefully a *desire* to find out more about you!

As you begin to develop your resumé, make sure to allow plenty of time to develop it. Plan to enlist several qualified proofreaders to check your work. We cannot stress strongly enough the need for your resumé to be perfect. A simple typo or misuse of grammar can disqualify you from the job of your dreams. Don't allow a lack of attention to detail to stand between you and your future career.

Further, your resumé must be 100 percent accurate and truthful. Do not fabricate information or fudge dates to make yourself look better. It will only come back to haunt you in the

GRADUATE *Quote*

Derwin Wallace
Graduate: Devry University and Keller Graduate
School of Management
Career: Director of Corporate Investor Relations
National Association of Investor Corps

In my position, my main responsibility is to put companies that trade in the stock market in front of investors in hopes they may purchase that company's stock. Just as my education gave me limitless opportunities, yours will too. Corporate America is a battlefield and you must get your armor ready. Your education is your preparation for battle—it is your boot camp for the real world.

When you land your new position, live below your means. Doing this gives you freedom. If you buy that BMW, the designer clothes, and the mansion on a hill and all of your money goes to pay the bills, you have lost your freedom and flexibility—you're a slave to a paycheck. The major stressor in life is to be tied to a job that you hate and can't leave because without it you will lose all your material possessions.

long run. Dennis Reina, organizational psychologist and author of *Trust and Betrayal in the Workplace,* states, "I think that what you put in a resumé absolutely has to be rock-solid, concrete, and verifiable. If there are any questions, it will immediately throw both your application and your credibility into question" (Dresang, 2007). People have been fired from positions after they were hired because they misrepresented themselves on their resumés, cover letters, or applications.

As you begin to build your resumé, remember to "call in the **D.O.C.T.O.R.**"

D: Design

Visual **design** and format are imperative to a successful resumé. You need to think about the font that you plan to use; whether color is appropriate (usually, it is not); the use of bullets, lines, or shading; and where you are going to put information. You also need to pay attention to the text balance on the page (centered left/right, top/bottom). The visual aspect of your resumé will be the first impression. "Make it pretty" (Britton-Whitcomb, 2003).

O: Objective

Writing a clear and specific **objective** can help get your foot in the door. The reader, usually your potential employer, needs to be able to scan your resumé and gather as much detail as possible as quickly as possible. A job-specific objective can help. Consider the following two objectives:

- **Vague objective:** To get a job as an elementary school teacher in the Dallas Area School District.
- **Specific objective:** To secure an elementary teaching position that will enable me to use my 14 years of creative teaching experience, curriculum development abilities, supervisory skills, and commitment to superior instruction in a team environment.

C: Clarity

Clarity is of paramount importance, especially when including your past responsibilities, education, and job responsibilities. Be certain that you let the reader know exactly what you have done, what specific education you have gained, and what progress you have made. Being vague and unclear can cost you an interview.

T: Truth

When writing your resumé, you may be tempted to fudge a little bit here and there to make yourself look better. Perhaps you were out of work for a few months and you think it looks bad to have this gap in your chronological history. Avoid the urge to fudge. Telling the absolute **truth** on a resumé is essential. A lie, even a small one, can (and usually will) come back to haunt you.

O: Organization

Before you begin your resumé, think about the **organization** of your data. We will provide a model resumé; however, there are several other formats you might select. It is most important that you present your information in an attractive, easy-to-read, comprehensive format.

R: Review

Reviewing your resumé and cover letter is important, but having someone else review them for clarity, accuracy, spelling, grammar, formatting, and overall content can be one of the best things you can do for your job search.

The basic tips in Figure 7.5 will help you as you begin building a dynamic resumé. Some other basic tips include the following:

- Do not date stamp or record the preparation date of your resumé in any place.
- Limit your resumé (and cover letter) to one page each (a two-page resumé is appropriate if you have more than 10 years of experience).
- Use standard resumé paper colors, such as white, cream, gray, or beige.
- Use bullets (such as these) to help profile lists.
- Avoid fancy or hard-to-read fonts.
- Use a standard font size between 10 and 14 points.
- Do not staple anything to your resumé (or cover letter).
- Try to avoid the use of *I, me,* or *my* in your resumé (if you must use them, do so sparingly).
- Avoid contractions such as *don't,* and do not use abbreviations.
- Use action verbs such as *designed, managed, created, recruited, simplified,* and *built.*

Figure 7.5 General Inclusion Tips

Contact information (name, complete mailing address, phone and cell numbers, fax number, e-mail address, webpage URL)	MUST include
Education, degrees, certificates, advanced training (to include dates and names of degrees)	MUST include
Current and past work history, experience and responsibilities	MUST include
Past accomplishments (this is *not* the same as work history or responsibilities)	MUST include
Specific licensures	MUST include
Specific career objective (different for each position for which you apply)	SHOULD include
Summary or list of qualifications, strengths, specializations	SHOULD include
Special skills (including special technical skills or multiple language skills)	SHOULD include
Volunteer work, public service, and/or community involvement	SHOULD include
Internships, externships, and/or extracurricular activities	SHOULD include
Awards, honors, certificates of achievement, special recognitions (at work or in the community)	SHOULD include
Military experience	CONSIDER including
Professional/preprofessional memberships, affiliations, and/or associations	CONSIDER including
Publications and presentations	CONSIDER including
Current business phone number and/or address (where you are working at the moment)	DO NOT include
Availability (date/time to begin work)	DO NOT include
Geographic limitations	DO NOT include
Personal hobbies or interests	DO NOT include
Personal information such as age, sex, health status, marital status, parental status, ethnicity, or religious affiliation	DO NOT include
Photos	DO NOT include
Salary requirements or money issues	DO NOT include (unless specifically asked to provide a salary history)
References	DO NOT include unless specifically asked but have the information ready on a separate sheet of paper that matches your resumé

- Avoid the use of full sentences; fragments are fine on a resumé, but not in a cover letter.

- Use the correct verb tense. You will use past tense (such as *recruited*), except when referring to your current job.

- Do not include irrelevant information that does not pertain to this particular job search.

- Choose a format that puts your "best foot" or greatest assets forward.

Remember that the job market is highly competitive. Your job is to write a resumé that is solid, appealing, comprehensive, and brief. The idea is to get someone to read it and make him or her want to know more about you.

BUILDING YOUR RESUMÉ

What Are the Major Differences?

There are different types of resumés, but primarily they can be classified as chronological resumés, functional resumés, accomplishment resumés, or a combination of the three. Your job package may also contain a portfolio. You might consider submitting a video resumé or a resumé that can be easily scanned and sent electronically. Each is described below.

- A **chronological resumé** organizes education and work experience in reverse chronological order (your last or present job is listed first).

- A **functional resumé** organizes your work and experience around specific skills and duties.

- An **accomplishment resumé** allows you to place your past accomplishments into categories that are not necessarily associated with an employer, but shows your track record of "getting the job done." This type of resumé is usually reserved for those with previous work experience.

- A **video resumé** is a resumé that showcases your experiences and talent through a brief (three- to five-minute) video recording. A video resumé is often used to supplement a traditional resumé and shows your creative and technological skills. Some employers will not accept video resumés because they can lead to claims of bias.

- A **scannable resumé** is a resumé with very little formatting and a clear font such as Courier, Arial, or Times New Roman. These resumés may appear to be less visually appealing, but they are easier to read once scanned. You may be asked to send your resumé as a PDF. A PDF file basically takes a snapshot of your document exactly as it was prepared and ensures that your electronic resumé remains just as you designed it.

- An **electronic (or plain text) resumé** is one that can be easily sent online and scanned electronically for *keywords and skills* based on the company's needs and job advertisement. It is saved in American Standard Code for Information Interchange (ASCII) format. When designing your electronic resumé, consider the spacing, formatting, and fonts. Avoid italics, bullets (use asterisks instead), and columns. Align the text on the left. Do not indent with tabs or use parentheses or brackets. To save your current or future resumé as an electronic or plain text resumé, simply click "Save as" and in the "Save as type" box, select "Plain Text." Then re-open your file and make adjustments, corrections, and additions.

- A *portfolio* is a binder, website, CD-ROM, flash drive, or cloud file that showcases your very best work. It details your projects, awards, certificates, certifications, degrees, transcripts, military experience, and major accomplishments. Your portfolio should always be specific to the position for which you are applying.

FIRST NAME and LAST NAME
Street Address, City, State Zip Code
(803) 555-5555
Jdoe@email.sc.edu

OBJECTIVE or SUMMARY
A brief, industry-focused statement that may be omitted when resume is accompanied by a cover letter.

EDUCATION

University of South Carolina   Columbia, SC
Bachelor of Science   May 2015
Major: Sport and Entertainment Management
Emphasis: (or Concentration and/or Minor if applicable)
GPA: (optional if 3.0 or above, or Major GPA)
Honors: Academic related awards/recognitions

Study Abroad (if applicable)   Location

PROFESSIONAL EXPERIENCE (listed in reverse chronological order)

Employer/Company Name   City, State
Title of position held   Month Year – Month Year
Compose 1-2 sentences describing the role of the position that you held. This should be an overview of the job and not a list of duties. Avoid using pronouns (I, you, me, my, they, he, etc.).
- Use an action verb to begin 2 to 4 statements of accomplishments.
- Indicate knowledge developed, transferable skills and accomplishments/abilities.
- Use quantitative descriptions (#, $, %) to add strength to your statements.
- Prioritize statements by importance and relevance to the position you are applying.

Employer/Company Name   City, State
Title of position held   Month Year – Month Year
Compose 1-2 sentences describing the role of the position that you held. This should be an overview of the job and not a list of duties. Avoid using pronouns (I, you, me, my, they, he, etc.).
- Use an action verb to begin 2 to 4 statements of accomplishments.
- Indicate knowledge developed, transferable skills and accomplishments/abilities.
- Use quantitative descriptions (#, $, %) to add strength to your statements.
- Prioritize statements by importance and relevance to the position you are applying.

Employer/Company Name   City, State
Title of position held   Month Year – Month Year
Compose 1-2 sentences describing the role of the position that you held. This should be an overview of the job and not a list of duties. Avoid using pronouns (I, you, me, my, they, he, etc.).
- Use an action verb to begin 2 to 4 statements of accomplishments.
- Indicate knowledge developed, transferable skills and accomplishments/abilities.
- Use quantitative descriptions (#, $, %) to add strength to your statements.

SKILLS   Include IT, foreign language, and industry-related software. Indicate proficiency levels.
                 (iIT majors may want to move their IT Skills section to follow the Education section)

AWARDS   Include any non-academic, job-related awards or recognitions.

ACTIVITIES   Industry-specific memberships or relevant activities (student organizations, volunteer, leadership positions).

FIRST NAME and LAST NAME
Street Address, City, State Zip Code
(803) 555-5555
Jdoe@email.sc.edu

Professional References

Current Supervisor: Jimny Cricket, Team Leader
SCANA Corporation
2020 Operation Way
Cayce, SC 29169
803-XXX-XXXX

Past Supervisor: Joseph Doe, Dean
University of South Carolina
102 Osborne Admin Building
Columbia, SC 29208
803-XXX-5555

Past Supervisor: Peter Pan, Manager
Disney, Inc.
125 Fairdust Road
West Columbia, SC 29073
803-555-5555

Past Supervisor: Susan Bones, Professor
Hogwarts School
123 Green Street
Columbia, SC 29208
803-999-9999

Job Search & Resume Workshop
The Marnie Pearce Professionalism Program

1. Identify personal characteristics to effectively interact with internal and external environments.
2. Develop a professional attitude and image.
3. Design a strategic career plan and create necessary documents to obtain career goals.
5. Identify potential questions and concerns for future interview situations.
6. Develop effective communication skills, verbal and non-verbal, for the workplace.
8. Investigate resources to assist in professional development.
10. Participate in professional development activities that ensure a smooth transition into the workplace.

With the people sitting around you, discuss and answer each of these job search questions.

1) What do YOU have to offer a prospective employer?
-
-
-

2) What is your target? Location, type of companies, positions and qualifications?
-
-
-

3) Who is on your list? Have you prioritized the list?
-
-
-

Resume Peer Review
Evaluator #1 (print name) _____

Evaluator #2 (print name) _____

Evaluator #3 (print name) _____

Print Your Name _____

chapter eight

INTERVIEW

INTERVIEWING LIKE A PRO

The best career advice to give anyone is this:
"Find out what you like doing best and
get someone to pay you for doing it."
—Katherine Whitehorn

THE BIG DAY IS HERE

How Do You Make the Impression of a Lifetime?

Remember the *eight-second rule* for making an impression. Consider this: During the interview process, you have even less. A judgment is made immediately about you: your dress, your grooming, your stance, your handshake, and your overall visual impression. Right or wrong, the interviewer will form an immediate first opinion of you—just as you will form an immediate first impression of your interviewer.

There are several ways your potential employer might choose to conduct the interview. In today's globally connected world, the standard face-to-face interview may not be the first choice of an employer—especially if the company has to pay to have you visit the office. Your interview may be conducted in one of the following ways:

- **In Person.** This type of interview takes place face-to-face with one person or with a group of people. The interview usually happens at the place of business.
- **Electronic.** With so many electronic ways to communicate, some employers are using the Internet to interview potential employees through Skype, GoToMeeting, WebEx, or other networking sites.
- **Social.** You may have an interview where you are asked to join the members of the interview team at a restaurant or outside the business location.
- **Phone.** Because of the high cost of bringing in someone to an interview, many employers will conduct the first interview over the phone. If you do well and the company is impressed, you will be brought in for an in-person interview.

As you begin to prepare for your interview, consider the following mnemonic. If you confidently carry R.E.W.A.R.D.S. with you to an interview, you will most likely get rewards after the interview, such as a job offer, benefits, and a career in which you can grow and prosper.

R: Rapport

Rapport is basically your "relationship" (intended or unintended) with another person—the emotional alliance you establish with someone. Consider how you come across to others. Rapport involves your verbal and nonverbal communication efforts. You should strive to establish a positive relationship with potential employers and future colleagues.

E: Education and Training

Be confident about what you know, and eloquently promote your abilities, skills, and talents to the interviewer. Remember, if you don't promote yourself, it is unlikely that anyone else will.

W: Willingness

Project a sense of willingness to learn new things, to become a team member, to assist the company with growth and new projects, and to keep up with advancements and changes in the modern world of work. Potential employers enjoy seeing an attitude of willingness and engagement.

Would you be more comfortable with a face-to-face, electronic, social, or phone interview? Why?

Shutterstock

A: Appearance

Dress for success. Pay close attention to your grooming, your hygiene, your hair, your clothing, and yes, even your shoes and socks (or hosiery). It all matters—and it is all noticed. Never make the mistake of thinking that appearance is not important. You will also want to consider dressing for a specific type of job. Careers in health studies may require a different type of interview dress than careers in aviation maintenance, engineering, or business.

R: Response

Project positivity and optimism in your responses to the questions asked in the interview. Even if you have to talk about your weaknesses or past experiences of conflict and turmoil, put a positive spin on them. Let the interviewer know that you have learned from adversity.

D: Demeanor

Cast a quality of confidence (not cockiness), intelligence, professionalism, and positivity. Carrying yourself with confidence during the interview will not go unnoticed. Pay attention to your handshake, eye contact, posture, mannerisms, and facial expressions.

S: Sincerity

No one likes phony people, especially a potential employer. Be yourself and strive to be sincere in your answers, your emotions, and your passion.

PREPARING FOR THE INTERVIEW

What Steps Can I Take to Ensure Success?

Just as you prepared for exams, you will need to prepare for the interview. Please do not make the common mistake of thinking that your degree or past work experience will get you the job. It may, but more often than you would believe, it is the interview and the relationship that you establish that day that gets you the offer. Your experience and credentials are important, but nothing is more important than how well you are prepared for this day and how well you represent yourself. As you prepare for your interview, consider the following sound advice.

Days Before the Interview

- Prepare extra copies of your resumé to take to the interview. Though one person typically conducts interviews, some employers designate several people to sit in on the interview process.

- Place your extra resumés, references, and other job search information in a professional portfolio (leather binder) or nice folder. Avoid carrying loose papers and never carry a backpack to an interview.

- Prepare a typed reference sheet and take several copies to the interview.

- If achievement portfolios are required, update your portfolio with any last-minute, applicable information.

- Using the research that you have done on the company, make a list of questions that you want to ask the interviewer. Never attend an interview without asking questions yourself. You are interviewing them just as they are interviewing you. Interviewers are much more impressed if they think you have researched the company and have questions to ask.

- Have a friend or colleague sit with you and ask questions that you might anticipate. Have this person throw a few "surprise questions" your way, too.

- Ask someone whose opinion you trust to look at your interview outfit and give you advice and suggestions for improvement.

- Make sure you know how to get to the interview site. Make a dry run if you have to. Being late for your interview will be the "kiss of death" for that job.

- Check the night before to make certain that you have transportation and that all of your personal needs are met, such as child care.

- Be sure you have enough gas to reach your destination if you are driving yourself. What is the availability for parking? Will you need to allow time for finding a parking place?

> *Nothing splendid has ever been achieved except by those who dared believe that something inside them was superior to circumstance.*
> —Bruce Barton

The Day of the Interview

- Get up early and spend some time alone reviewing the job announcement, your resumé, your portfolio, the company's profile, and other important information.

- Bring a pen, paper, and calendar with you to the interview. These can be kept in your portfolio, too.

- Know where your items are located so that you do not have to search for them during an interview. Fumbling around makes you look disorganized and unprepared.

- Prepare for the unknown: Take an umbrella, even if it is sunny; leave your home early, even though the interview site is only a few miles away; and so on.

- Be certain that your clothes are clean and pressed.

- Be certain that your shoes are spotless and shined.

- Be certain that you are groomed and that your breath is fresh. Breath mints or sprays go a long way.

- Arrive at the interview at least 15 minutes early.

- If you are a smoker, *do not* smoke in the car on the way to the interview and try to avoid smoking in your interview clothes. Often, the smell of cigarette smoke lingers for hours and clings to your clothing. For many, this is an immediate turn-off. Some employers will find a way not to hire a smoker because of increased insurance premiums paid for smokers.

- Do not carry any type of food or drink into the interview with you.

- Do not chew gum during the interview.

- Before you enter the building, turn off your cell phone, pager, Blackberry, iPod, tablet, or any other electronic device except your hearing aid, pacemaker, or other life-assisting device. *Turn them off.* Period! There is no excuse for your cell phone to ring during an interview. No one, including you, is that important.

- Do not take anyone with you to the interview unless the person remains in the car. Under no circumstances should you take anyone with you into the building!

During the Interview

- Establish eye contact.
- Work to develop an immediate rapport.
- Offer a firm handshake to everyone in the room.
- Pay close attention to your posture (straight shoulders, positive stride, etc.).
- Speak with clarity and enunciate your words.
- Ask where to sit if you are not told.
- Enter with a positive and upbeat attitude.
- Jot down the names of everyone in the room as they are introduced to you. You may even draw an impromptu seating chart to remind you of who's who in the room.
- Refer to people by their names if you address them during the interview.
- Take notes during the interview.
- Answer every question asked, as long as the question is legal.
- You don't have to be deadly serious or stodgy, but it is advisable to avoid jokes or off-color humor during the interview process.
- Consider your grammar and strive to use correct speech.
- If you need clarification on a question, ask for it before you begin your answer.
- Never degrade or talk badly about a past job or employer. This will only come back to haunt you.
- If at all possible, do not discuss any aspect of your personal life such as children, marriage, or family.
- During the interview, jot down any questions that may arise that you did not already consider.
- If you are offered anything to eat or drink, accept only water, just in case your mouth becomes dry during the interview.
- Never ask about money or company benefits during an interview, especially during the first interview, unless the interviewer approaches the topic. Let him or her lead this discussion. If you are asked about salary requirements, respond with this question: "What is the range for this job?" In negotiations of any kind, you want the other person to offer information first. If you think you are highly qualified, respond with a salary amount close to the top of the range by saying, "Based on my qualifications and experience, I would consider a salary of $_____."
- Strive to never appear desperate or "begging" for the job. There is a difference between excitement and desperation.

After the Interview

- Shake hands with everyone in the room and thank them for the opportunity to meet with them. Let them know that you were honored to have the opportunity. Humility goes a long way.
- Politely let them know that you enjoyed the interview and that you are very interested in the position.
- Ask each person in the room for a business card. This provides you with their correct name spelling, address, and e-mail address for use in future correspondence.
- Don't linger around the site unless you are told to wait. This makes you look desperate.
- Always follow up with a personalized thank you note.

What preparations do you need to make to arrive at the interview on time?

Shutterstock

General Tips

- Remember the cardinal rule of interviewing: Interviewers are not interested in what the company can do for you; they are interested in what you can do for the company. Therefore, you must present your case on why you want to work for the company and the contributions you are prepared to make.

- Be truthful in every aspect of the job search: the application, your resumé, your cover letter, your portfolio, your references, your question responses, your salary history, and yes, your interest in the position.

- Be nice and gracious to everyone you meet. You never know which person will be the one to interview you.

DRESSING FOR SUCCESS

What Do I Wear to My Interview?

This is tricky because there is no general, "one size fits all" answer. A person interviewing for a position at a bank or hospital might dress differently than a person who is applying at maintenance shop or small computer business. Even if you know that the workplace to which you are applying has a casual dress policy, dress up for your interview. Dressing well suggests that you take the interview seriously and that you planned in advance. One overriding rule is when you are in doubt about how to dress, always be more conservative than trendy and always be clean and neat. Any business will appreciate this. And remember, your appearance speaks as loudly as you do and projects a lasting, visual image. Figure 8.1 outlines a few general guidelines for interview attire.

> *If you follow your bliss, doors will open for you that wouldn't have opened for anyone else.*
>
> —Joseph Campbell

ANTICIPATING THE INTERVIEWER'S QUESTIONS

Can You Answer Hard Questions with a Positive Attitude?

Richard Nelson Bolles, author of *What Color Is Your Parachute?* (2011), the most widely published job-hunting book in history with over 10 million copies in print, makes an astounding assertion. He states, "You don't have to spend hours memorizing a lot of 'good answers' to potential questions from the employer. There are only five questions that matter." Wow. Five questions!

With this statement, do not think that you will only be asked five questions. Rather, Mr. Bolles is suggesting that with every question asked of you, the interviewer is trying to get to the heart of the matter—the five basic questions are:

1. Why are you here?
2. What can you do for us?
3. What kind of person are you?
4. What distinguishes you from the 19 other people who can do the same tasks that you can?
5. Can I afford you?

So, how do interviewers get to "the heart of the matter"? How do they pull the answers to these five questions from you? Ironically, they do it by asking many, many other questions. This section will offer you insight into some common and not-so-common questions asked by today's employers.

Figure 8.1 General Tips for Successful Interview Attire

Item	Women	Men
Hair	Always clean and dry; pulled away from the face	Always clean and dry; pulled in a ponytail if you have long hair and trimmed neatly
Nails	Well manicured; clear polish is best; do not use wild colors or decorative designs	Clean and clipped
Tattoos	Cover them for the interview	Cover them for the interview
Teeth/Dentures	Always clean; use mouthwash; take a breath mint	Always clean; use mouthwash; take a breath mint
Perfume/Cologne/ Aftershave/Smells	Wear sparingly or none at all; never smoke before an interview	Wear sparingly or none at all; never smoke before an interview
Makeup	Wear sparingly and in good taste; don't overdo it	N/A
Clothes	Clean, pressed, conservative, coordinated, and traditionally a dark color; no jeans; no tight-fitting, body-hugging outfits; a dark, conservative suit is always appropriate	Clean, pressed, conservative; white long-sleeved shirts with collar; khakis or dress slacks with a belt matching your shoes; no jeans; dry-cleaned navy blue, grey, or black suit (with tie and belt) if appropriate
Shoes	Appropriate for your outfit but always clean and polished; avoid stiletto heels and open-toed shoes; always wear neutral hosiery	Appropriate for your outfit, but always clean and polished; black shoes are preferred; avoid tennis shoes; wear socks that match your shoes, not your pants
Jewelry	Avoid excessive jewelry; choose classic over trendy; remove any jewelry-adorned piercings except stud earrings; no hoop or 6" drop earrings; no dangling bracelets; experts say no jewelry is better than "cheap" jewelry; preferably gold or silver	Avoid excessive jewelry; no gold chains; remove any jewelry-adorned piercings
Accessories	Handbag (plain leather is preferable); nice portfolio; no visible cell phone (make sure it is off)	Nice portfolio; no visible cell phone (make sure it is off)

It is usually customary that the interviewer will make "small talk" for a few minutes to give you time to relax and get comfortable. You should avoid answering questions with a simple yes or no. Briefly elaborate on your answers without talking too much. For example, if the interviewer says, "I hope you had no trouble finding our building," you should not just answer "No." You might say something like, "Not at all. I live near here so I was familiar with the location," or "Actually, I had a part-time job when I was a sophomore and I brought materials to one of your managers from my department manager."

Interviewers will often say to you, "Tell me about yourself." They are not looking for your life history as much as they are gathering background information on you and observing how well you can present information. Provide highlights of your education, experience, and accomplishments. If you are just yourself and enjoy the process, this will show.

The interviewer might then ask you, "What do you know about our company?" This is a good opportunity for you to show how prepared you are. You could open your portfolio and tell

GRADUATE *Quote*

Brayton Williams
Graduate!
The University of Nevada, Las Vegas
Career: Hotel Management

... that I learned about interviewing is to begin ... sional interview years before it occurs. It is ... ntage of internships, volunteer, join clubs, and ... organizations. I learned that it was important ... m. Stacking your resumé with activities that ... ooked on favorably by any employer.

... ing the company, I found some interesting facts on your ... national company based in New York and that you have ... you have several divisions including food processing and ... food sales. In fact, this information is the reason I applied ... Center. My minor in college is restaurant management, ... at place to put my knowledge and the skills to great use."

... your answer to your own situation. There is no way to ... ns an interviewer may ask. The key is to have anticipated ... comfortable with the message you want to convey about ... decisive. As you talk, remember to look at the interviewer ... cates that you are listening intently.

... ch-other" session, you can anticipate more direct and ... common questions that you might expect include:

... company and in the position?

... r in _____?

... ar activities.

... ence? Why?

- Are you willing to travel?
- Do you have job experience in _____?
- What can you do for the company?
- What other companies are you interviewing with?
- Tell me about a difficult problem you had and how you solved it.
- Tell me about a time when you worked under stress.
- What kind of accomplishment gives you the greatest satisfaction?
- What are your long- and short-range goals?
- Where do you see yourself in five years?

> *Never wear a backward baseball cap to an interview unless you are interviewing for the job of umpire.*
>
> —Dan Zevin

- What one word best describes you?
- How do you deal with difficult people?
- Describe one goal you set over the past six months and how you went about accomplishing it.
- What is the biggest mistake you ever made? What did you learn from it?
- What subject in school gave you the most challenges? Why?
- What past experiences or courses have prepared you for this position?
- Would you prefer to work alone or with a group of people? Why?

Some more in-depth and less common questions might be:

- What type of manager would bring out the best in you? Why?
- What is the most important thing to you in a job? Why?
- Who has been the most influential person in your life? Why?
- If I called your past supervisor, how would he or she describe you?
- In what area do you lack the most confidence?
- In what area of this position do you lack the most experience? How do you plan to accommodate for this?
- If you could design your own job evaluation form with only five qualities to be evaluated, what five qualities would you list? Why?
- Tell us about a time when you put your best forward and the end result was still unfavorable. Why do you think this happened? What did you do about it? What did you learn from the situation?
- What is the biggest change to which you have ever had to adapt? What strategies did you employ to adjust to this change?
- How do you effectively deal with interpersonal conflicts?
- How do you effectively deal with miscommunication?
- How do you effectively deal with gossip?
- Of what are you most proud in your professional life? Why?
- If you could not be involved in this job or profession any longer, what would you do for a vocation? Why? Why are you not doing that now?

Regardless of the question asked, your primary responsibility in the interview is to be straightforward and honest and to answer the question to the very best of your ability.

Look over the position advertisement, the company's website, and your own application materials and think about questions that may be asked of you. Write down five questions that you might anticipate that are not listed above.

1. _____

2. _____

3. _____

4. _____

5. _____

ASK INFORMED QUESTIONS

Am I Allowed to Interview the Interviewer?

You should feel free to ask the interviewer questions during the interview, but the interviewer should lead the majority of the first part of the interview. At the close of the interview, you may be asked if you have any questions. If this opportunity is not offered, you should say, "I have a few questions, if you don't mind." Asking questions of the interviewer is impressive and indicates that you are interviewing them as well. Some typical questions follow:

- How would you describe a typical day in this position?
- What kind of training can I anticipate?
- What is the probationary period of employment?
- What are the opportunities for personal growth and professional development?
- To whom would I report?
- Will I have an opportunity to meet some of my coworkers?
- Would you describe the training program?
- When will my first job performance evaluation take place?
- Why do you enjoy working for this company?
- How would you describe the most successful person working at this company? Why?
- What objectives do you expect to be met by your new employee in the first six months?
- Can you tell me about an assignment I might be asked to do?
- What happened to the person who most recently held this position?
- What do you see as the major challenges facing this organization? Why?
- How would you describe the culture of the workplace in this organization?
- What does this company value?

ROUGH, TOUGH, HARD QUESTIONS

How Do You Effectively Manage Inappropriate or Illegal Questions?

Sadly, you may encounter questions that are inappropriate or even illegal. Remember, federal and state laws may prohibit many questions that deal with your personal life, and federal laws such as the Civil Rights Act of 1964 and the Americans with Disabilities Act of 1990 do regulate certain questions that can be asked during an interview, but some employers may still ask inappropriate and illegal questions.

BIGGEST INTERVIEW *Blunders*

Margaret's interview outfit was flawless. Her suit was immaculate, her blouse was beautiful and well-coordinated, her shoes were polished, and her hair and makeup were salon-quality. She had prepared for the interview days in advance and even got a friend of hers to quiz her on many different interview questions. Margaret made two huge errors, however. She arrived a few minutes late. And even though she was dressed to the nines, to calm her nerves, she smoked two cigarettes in the car on the way to the interview. Mrs. Compton, the interviewer, immediately noticed the smell, and this began the interview on a negative note. However, the worst was yet to come. Upon being seated in Mrs. Compton's office, Margaret reached into her purse and pulled out a Red Bull. "I'm running late this morning," she said. "I need to have a shot of energy."

Margaret answered the questions well and did not stumble on any responses. She had the education for which they were looking and she was polite and confident. However, the two strikes at the beginning of the interview were hard to overcome. At the end of the interview, Margaret's cell phone rang and she answered it. *Strike three.*

LESSON: A part of interviewing is respecting the person who is conducting the interview by showing up on time and giving him or her your undivided attention. Regardless of what you did or did not eat for breakfast, you would never pull out food or beverage during an interview. Leave your cell phone in the car or at home. You've worked too hard to have a ringing phone cost you your dream job—and it will.

How do you plan to handle questions that may be illegal to ask?

Shutterstock

If illegal or inappropriate questions are asked in person or on an application, it can be challenging to manage them and still retain your composure and decorum. It is up to you how much you want to tell a potential employer about your personal life or lifestyle, and they cannot demand an answer unless the question is in direct relationship to the job for which you applied, such as certain jobs in aviation and service industry jobs where alcohol is served.

First, review the list of questions that many experts consider illegal, or at best inappropriate, and later in this section, we will discuss how to respond if you are asked an illegal or unethical question.

With some exceptions, such as religious organizations, employers should not ask you about:

- **Your age.** You should generally not be asked this question. However, some professions are age-restricted (such as airline pilots and bartending) and this question is perfectly legal.

- **Your marital status, your parental status, or your living situation (who lives with you or why).** If you are asked this question, the employer is really trying to find out if you will be at work on a regular basis or if you can travel. It is legal to ask, "Does your personal schedule permit extensive travel?" but it is not legal to ask, "Would you get into trouble with your wife or children if you were asked to travel a lot?" It is illegal to ask if you are planning a family, if you are pregnant, or if you have ever had an abortion.

- **Your race or national origin.** You should not be asked about either of these categories, nor should you ever be asked to provide a photo of yourself. However, every employer can, on employment, ask that you provide legal documentation that you are eligible and clear to work in the United States. At this point, an employer can also ask for a photograph for security and identification purposes.

- **Your sexual orientation.** This is tricky, but generally it is still legal (albeit unethical) for a potential employer to ask about your sexual orientation. It is up to you if you choose to answer this question. Some interviewers try to get at this answer by asking about your marital status, which is illegal to ask.

- **Your religious affiliation.** This question is illegal and should never be asked. However, if you are asked this question, the interviewer is probably trying to determine if your religion might prevent you from working on weekends, Sundays, or certain holidays. It is legal to ask, "Would you be willing to work on Sunday?" or "Would you be willing to work on Christmas?"

- **Your political affiliation.** It is legal to ask this question; however, "Some states ban discrimination on this basis and political affiliation may not be used for discriminatory purposes in federal-government employment" (Smith, 2007).

- **Your physical, mental, or emotional limitations.** You cannot be asked a question such as, "Have you ever been treated for depression or any mental illness?" but you can be asked a question such as, "This position requires that you deal with many stressful situations and many situations in which you will encounter conflict. Do you feel that you have any limitations that might prevent you from managing these situations effectively?" It is never legal to ask about your HIV status, your disabilities, or any prescription drugs that you may take.

- **Your physical attributes.** You cannot be asked questions about your height or weight unless this is directly tied to job performance due to specific, predetermined limitations.

- **Your financial status.** An employer cannot ask you if have a checking or savings account, how much money you save each month, or any question about your credit rating. However, many states do allow potential employers to run credit checks on applicants and potential employees.

- **Your personal habits.** Generally, employers can ask if you smoke at home, but this question has led to some lawsuits. "Currently, 31 states ban policies prohibiting off-duty smoking" (Smith, 2007).

- **Your arrest status.** Your arrest status is completely different from your conviction status. It *is* legal to ask if you have ever been convicted of a crime. A few states do allow an employer to ask if you have been arrested if it is job related.

- **Your affiliations.** It is not legal to ask you to which organizations you belong, except for certain professional organizations (such as The National Association of Architects if you are applying for a position in the architectural field). An employer, cannot, however, ask if you belong to the Shriners, Freemasons, or any union.

- **Your military status.** You may not be asked what type of discharge you had from the military. You should not be asked if you ever belonged to the military unless it is job related.

- **Your school and/or college records.** School and college records may be sought only with your consent. Usually, you have to order the official transcript and have it sent directly to your employer.

Basically it comes down to money. It is very expensive to hire, train, and retain an employee in today's workforce. An employer wants to know as much about you as possible—basically, they want to know if you are qualified, if you will get along with others, and if you will be at work when you say you will be there.

So, how do you handle questions that may be illegal or inappropriate? This can be tricky at best and "the kiss of death" at worst. Consider this: Can an employer ask you if you are married? No, they cannot. However, if this type of question arises, you can always view it as a positive moment. You might respond: "Yes, I am married and my spouse and I fully support each other's careers and advancement possibilities."

Can an employer ask, "Are you gay?" Generally, yes, but again, you have to decide how you would answer this question (whether the answer is yes or no). If you are uncomfortable with this question, you may respond, "Before I answer that question, can you discuss how this is related to this particular position?" or "I choose not to answer that question based on my personal beliefs."

Sometimes, you will have to do an evaluation of the employer. You may need to ask yourself, "Do I really want to work for a company that would ask an illegal or inappropriate question?" Ultimately, the choice is yours.

As an exercise, choose one area above and pretend that you were asked a question that was illegal, inappropriate, or taboo. State the question; then give your response to this question.

Anderson Ross/Picture Arts/BrandX/Jupiter

In the past, what preparations have served you best in getting ready for an interview?

POSITIVE HABITS
at Work

Work hard every day to become a true professional. Regardless of your profession, professionalism is a hallmark that employers seek in any employee. Professionalism includes things like helping without being asked, nurturing others who need assistance, representing your company with a positive attitude, avoiding gossip and hearsay, maintaining a strong ethical and moral base, managing the company's money well, using your time wisely, following company policy, and being a team player. If you learn how to do these things now, your current supervisor will not forget this when it comes time to write a letter of recommendation for you in the future.

Question:

_____

_____

My response:

_____

_____

_____

WIN, LOSE, OR DRAW, ALWAYS SAY THANK YOU IN WRITING

Do I Have to Say Thank You Even If I Don't Get the Job?

Indeed, it is safe to say that sending a thank you note is "the most overlooked step in the entire job search process" (Bolles, 2011). Yes, this is a mandatory step for every interview, and you

Figure 8.2 Thank You Note: After the Interview

CARSON SCOTT
1234 Lake Shadow Drive
Maple City, PA 12345
Scott@bl.com

January 20, 2013

Mr. James Pixler, RN
Director of Placement
Grace Care Center
123 Sizemore Street
Philadelphia, PA 12345

Dear Mr. Pixler,

Thank you for the wonderful opportunity to meet with you and the team at Grace Care Center on Monday. Your facilities are amazing, and the new wing is going to be a remarkable addition to your center.

I enjoyed learning more about the new position in Medical Assisting, and I think that my qualifications and experiences have prepared me for this challenging opportunity. I would consider it an honor to answer any further questions that you might have or to meet with you again if you consider it necessary.

I look forward to hearing from you at your convenience. If you need any additional information, you can reach me at 123-555-3454.

Thank you,

Carson Scott
CARSON SCOTT

must send one to every person who interviewed you. Period. In today's world of high-tech and run, run, run, this one act will set you apart from the thousands who interview on a daily basis. And yes, you must send a thank you letter even if you do not get the job. "When do I send the thank you note?" you might ask. ***Immediately after the interview.***

Sending a simple thank you note does many things. It lets the employer know that you have good manners, that you respect other people's time and efforts, that you are considerate, that you really do care about the position, and that you have positive people and communication skills. Yes, all of that from a card and stamp that can cost less than $2.00.

Figures 8.2 and 8.3 show examples of two thank you notes. Review them and consider using them as templates to build your own notes.

Figure 8.3 Thank You Note: After a Position Rejection

CARSON SCOTT
1234 Lake Shadow Drive
Maple City, PA 12345
Scott@bl.com

January 20, 2013

Mr. James Pixler, RN
Director of Placement
Grace Care Center
123 Sizemore Street
Philadelphia, PA 12345

Dear Mr. Pixler,

Thank you for the opportunity to meet with you and the team at Grace Care Center on Monday. I enjoyed learning more about your center and the planned addition.

While I was not offered the position, I did want to let you know that I appreciate your time, and I would like for you to contact me if you have any future openings where you feel my qualifications and experiences would match your needs. Grace is an incredible facility, and I would consider it an honor to hold a position there.

If you need to contact me in the future, you can reach me at 123-555-3454.

Thank you for your time and assistance, and good luck to you and your colleagues.

Sincerely,

Carson Scott
CARSON SCOTT

PUTTING IT ALL TOGETHER

Your chance to shine comes in many forms, such as your resumé and cover letter, but nothing speaks so loudly as **you** during an interview. Do not take this opportunity lightly. Just because the company is interested in you does not mean that you can glide through. Remember, there are countless people out there who are just as qualified and ready as you are. YOU have to sell you, and the interview is the perfect place to close the sell.

As you reflect on this chapter, keep the following pointers in mind:

- Go to the interview prepared.
- Practice interview questions with your friends or family.
- Anticipate illegal or probing questions.
- Ask informed questions of your interviewers.
- Dress for the interview like you want the job.
- Promote yourself. If you don't, no one will.

> *Job security is gone. The driving force must now come from the individual.*
>
> —Homa Bahrami

DIGITAL BRIEFCASE

SEARCHING FOR A POSITION

Search the Internet, newspaper, or corporate website and find a position for which you are (or soon will be) qualified. Send the ad to five friends on your social network and have them look at the company's website. Then have them formulate two questions each that may be asked by the interviewer from this company. Return your responses to the people who asked the question, and ask for feedback

REFERENCES

Bolles, R. (2011) *What color is your parachute? A practical manual for job hunters and career changers.* Berkeley, CA: Ten Speed Press.

Smith, R. (2007, August 14) Don't ask—maybe. Retrieved January 11, 2012, from www.forbes.com.

UNIVERSITY OF
SOUTH CAROLINA
College of Hospitality, Retail
and Sport Management

1. Identify personal characteristics to effectively interact with internal and external environments.
2. Develop a professional attitude and image.
3. Design a strategic career plan and create necessary documents to obtain career goals.
5. Identify potential questions and concerns for future interview situations.
6. Develop effective communication skills, verbal and non-verbal, for the workplace.
8. Investigate resources to assist in professional development.
10. Participate in professional development activities that ensure a smooth transition into the workplace.

Behavioral Interviewing—the STAR Method

<u>Situation</u>: Discuss a specific situation or problem that you encountered
<u>Task</u>: Explain the task that you had to complete or the ideas you used for resolving the problem
<u>Action:</u> Tell specific actions which you took, steps you followed, obstacles you had to overcome, etc.
<u>Results</u>: Highlight outcomes, goals achieved, accomplishments, etc.
Adapted from USC Career Center 2016

S - What was a Situation that relates to the question?

T - What were your Tasks?

A - What Action did you Take?

R - What was the Result?

Behavioral Interviewing Panel
The Marnie Pearce Professionalism Program

1. Identify personal characteristics to effectively interact with internal and external environments.
2. Develop a professional attitude and image.
3. Design a strategic career plan and create necessary documents to obtain career goals.
5. Identify potential questions and concerns for future interview situations.
6. Develop effective communication skills, verbal and non-verbal, for the workplace.
8. Investigate resources to assist in professional development.
10. Participate in professional development activities that ensure a smooth transition into the workplace.

Interview Preparation Exercise: Under each heading, cite examples of your own using the STAR method. Develop short stories around your experiences to describe your strengths and possible obstacles you had to overcome.

Behavioral Interviewing - Observation, Feedback

As the behavioral interview questions are asked, please evaluate the student volunteers as they interview. Did they deliver a well-organized and effective answer?

Situation?	Yes ☐ No ☐
Task?	Yes ☐ No ☐
Action?	Yes ☐ No ☐
Results?	Yes ☐ No ☐

What was good?

What could they have improved?

What area do I need to improve?

Teamwork
S
T
A
R

Communication Skills
S
T
A
R

Problem Solving Skills
S
T
A
R

Strong Work Ethic
S
T
A
R

Motivation and Initiative
S
T
A
R

Interpersonal Skills
S
T
A
R

Technical Skills
S
T
A
R

Organizational Skills
S
T
A
R

Flexibility /Adaptability Skills
S
T
A
R

Integrity
S
T
A
R

Print Your Name _____

167

chapter nine

PRIORITIZE

STRATEGIES FOR MANAGING PRIORITIES AND AVOIDING WORKPLACE LAND MINES

PART THREE: MANAGING YOUR CAREER

If you want to make good use of your time,
you've got to know what's most important
and then give it all you've got.
—Lee Iacocca

TIME—YOU HAVE ALL THERE IS

Can You Take Control of Your Life and Make the Most of Your Time?

You can definitely say four things about time: *It is fair. It does not discriminate. It treats everyone the same. Everyone has all there is.* No person has any more or less hours in a day than the next person. It may seem that Gary or Tamisha has more time than you do, but that's not the case. In a 24-hour span we all have 1440 minutes. No more. No less. There is one more thing you can definitely say about time, too: *It can be cruel and unrelenting.* It is one of the few things in our lives that we cannot stop. There are no time-out periods, no breaks, and try as we might, we can't turn it back, shut it down, or stop it. The good news, however, is that by learning how to manage our time more effectively, we don't need to slow it down or stop it. We can learn how to get things done and have more time for joy and fun.

So, how do you spend your time? Some people are very productive, whereas others scramble to find a few moments to enjoy life and have quality relationships. According to time management and personal productivity expert Donald Wetmore (2008), "The average working person spends less than two minutes per day in meaningful communication with their spouse or significant other and less than 30 seconds per day in meaningful communication with their children." Think about that for a moment. *Thirty seconds.* If you think that is amazing, consider the following list. As strange as it may seem, these figures are taken from the U.S. Bureau of Labor Statistics (2006). During your *working years* (age 20–65, a 45-year span) you spend an average of:

- 16 years sleeping
- 2.3 years eating
- 3.1 years doing housework
- 6 years watching TV
- 1.3 years on the telephone

This totals *28.7 years of your working life* doing things that you may not even consider in your time management plan. What happens to the remaining 16.3 years? Well, you will spend *14 of those years working*, which leaves you with 2.3 years, or only 20,000 hours during your working life, to embrace joy, spend time with your family, educate yourself, travel, and experience a host of other life-fulfilling activities. Dismal? Scary? It does not have to be. By learning how to manage your time, harness your energy and passion, and take control of your day-to-day activities, 2.3 years can be a long, exciting, productive time.

Why is it that some people seem to get so much more done than other people? They appear to always be calm and collected and have it together. Many people from this group work long hours in addition to going to school and taking care of a family. They never appear to be stressed out, and they seem to be able to do it all with grace and charm.

You are probably aware of others who are always late, never finish their projects on time, rarely seem to have time to get everything done, and appear to have no concrete goals for their lives. Sometimes, we get the idea that the first group accomplishes more because they have more time or because they don't have to work or they don't have children or they are smarter or have more help. Some of these reasons may be true, but in reality, many of them have learned how to overcome procrastination, tie their value system to their time management plan, and use their personal energy and passion to accomplish more.

"I can't do any more than I am doing right now," you may say to yourself. But is that really true? One of the keys to managing your time is to consider your values. What you value, enjoy, and love, you tend to put more passion, energy, and time toward. Do you value your family? If so, you make time for them. Do you value your friends? If so, you make time for them. Think about these questions: How much do you value having a career that you find fulfilling and rewarding? If you value your career, you will find time to devote toward making it successful. *We spend time on what we value!*

TIME MANAGEMENT AND SELF-DISCIPLINE

Do You Have What It Takes to "Git 'er Done"?

> *Self-discipline is teaching ourselves to do the things necessary to reach our goals without becoming sidetracked by bad habits.*
>
> —Denis Waitley

Time management is actually about managing you! It is about taking control and assuming responsibility for the time you are given on this earth. The sooner you understand and get control of how you use your time, the quicker you will be on your way to becoming successful in your career and many other activities. Learning to manage your time is a lesson that you will use in all aspects of your life. *You can't control time*, but you can control yourself. Time management is basically self-discipline—and self-discipline involves self-motivation

The word *discipline* comes from the Latin word meaning "to teach." Therefore, *self-discipline* is really about "teaching ourselves" (Waitley, 1997). Self-discipline implies that you have the ability to teach yourself how to get more done when things are going well and when they are not going so well. If you have self-discipline, you have learned how to hold it all together when things get tough, when you feel beaten, and when defeat seems just around the corner. It also means that when you have important tasks to complete, you can temporarily pull yourself away from enjoyable situations and fun times until those tasks are completed. Consider the chart in Figure 5.1 regarding self-discipline. **Self-discipline is really about four things**: **making choices, making changes, using willpower, and taking responsibility.**

Once you have made the *choice* to engage wholeheartedly in your work, stop procrastinating, and mange your time more effectively, you have to make the *changes* in your thoughts and behaviors to bring those choices to fruition. Then, you have to *accept responsibility* for your actions and take control of your life. You have to call on your *inner strength or willpower*—and you *do* have willpower. It may just be hidden or forgotten, but you do have it. You have the ability to empower yourself to get things done. No one can do this for you. You are responsible for your life and your actions. Self-discipline and willpower help you move in the direction of your dreams.

Willpower and self-discipline are all about *re-training your mind* to do what *you* want it to do and not what *it* wants to do. It is about eliminating the negative self-talk that so often derails us and causes us to procrastinate and get stressed out. By re-training your mind and resisting the urge to simply "obey" your subconscious, you are basically re-training your life. Consider the following situations:

- You come home from work, tired and weary, and you still have to finish a report for your boss by 8:00 a.m. tomorrow. Your subconscious mind tells you to sit down, put your feet up, and watch TV for a while. You have to tell your mind, "NO! I am going to take a short walk around the block to get my adrenaline flowing and then I'm going to write that report."

- You look at your desk or study space and you see all of the books and papers you have gathered for writing your report. Your subconscious mind tells you to just ig-

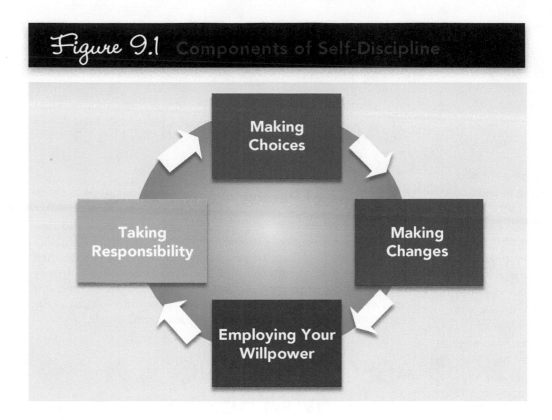

Figure 9.1 Components of Self-Discipline

nore it for a while; there's still time to get it done! You have to tell your mind, "ABSOLUTELY NOT! I'm going to get those materials organized and finish this report before I do anything else so I can get it off my back."

By re-training your mind and paying attention to your subconscious, you can teach yourself to develop the self-discipline and willpower to get things done and avoid the stress caused by procrastination. Willpower gives you strength to stay on track and avoid the guilt associated with putting things off or not doing them at all. Guilt turns to frustration, frustration turns to anger, and before you know it, your negative self-talk and subconscious mind have "won" and nothing gets done. You have the power to change this.

> *Begin doing what you want to do now. We are not living in eternity. We have only this moment, sparkling like a star in our hand and melting like a snowflake.*
>
> *—Marie B. Ray*

I'LL DO IT WHEN I HAVE A LITTLE FREE TIME

Is Time Really "Free"?

What is "free time" and when does it happen? We've all used that expression at one time or another: "I'll do that when I get a little more free time," or "I'm going to wait until I find a little more time." Can time be found? Is time free? Do we ever have a moment to call our own? The answer is "maybe," but free time has to be created by you, and it can only be created by getting the things done that must be completed for your success.

Free time is *not* time that you simply create by putting off work that needs to be done. Free time is *not* time that is spent procrastinating. Free time is *not* time that you take away from your duties, chores, studies, family, and obligations. That is **borrowed time,** and if you know the rules of good behavior, you know that anything you borrow, you must repay. When are you going

BIGGEST INTERVIEW
Blunders

Joaquim interviewed with a business owner of a large plumbing company. The owner interviewed him personally, explaining that he liked to know as much about every employee as possible. He gave Joaquim an intense interview. Joaquim thought he was doing very well until the owner asked him to take a pencil-and-paper test on managing priorities and handling stress. The test required him to prioritize 15 tasks and describe how he would get them accomplished in one day. Joaquim became very frustrated and stressed and finally told the owner that it was impossible to get the entire list done in one day. The owner responded, "This is a typical day's work for our associates; sometimes the work schedule is even heavier." The owner told Joaquim that he appeared to be an outstanding young man but recommended that he work as an apprentice until he learned to manage his time and priorities better.

LESSON: Try to be prepared for real-world activities that might be tested via simulations and other activities. Be sure to familiarize yourself with time and stress management techniques.

Time is the most valuable and most perishable of our possessions.

—John Randolph

to find the time to "repay" these blocks of time to yourself? Usually, you don't, and that is when and where you get into trouble and your stress level starts to rise. Free time *is* time that you reward yourself with when you have completed your studies, tasks, chores, and obligations.

PLANNING, DOODLING, OR BEGGING

What Type of Person Are You, Anyway?

We all have different personality types, but did you know we also have different time management personalities? Consider the list in Figure 9.2 explaining the different negative time management personalities. Respond YES or NO to each management style. Then, out to the side, explain why you think this type represents you and your daily thoughts on time, if it does. Then, in the last column, list at least one strategy that you can implement to overcome this type of negative time management style.

ABSOLUTELY NO . . . WELL, MAYBE

Do You Know How to Say No?

"No, I'm sorry, I can't do that," is perhaps one of the most difficult phrases you must learn to say when it comes to effective time management, but learning it is absolutely essential." If you continually say yes to everyone and every project, then quickly, you will have no time left for yourself, your family, your friends, and your projects. Many of us are taught from an early age that *no* is a bad word and that we should always try to avoid saying it to others. However, we are not taught that never saying "no" can cause us undue stress and feelings of guilt and frustration, as well as throw our time management plans into disarray. The word *no* needs to become a part of your everyday vocabulary. By learning to say "no" to a few things, you can begin to say "yes" to many other things—things that you want to do, things that you need to do, things that will help others in the long run, and goals and priorities at work that will help you get ahead. "No" is not rude; it is simply a way of managing your time so that you have more time to say "yes" to what is important and useful.

Learning to Say No: It's as Simple as Not Saying Yes

- Think before you answer out loud with an insincere or untrue "yes." Tell the person who is asking that you need time to think about it because you are already stretched pretty thin. Don't make an immediate decision. Buy yourself some time to think before you take on something that is going to stress you.

- Make sure you understand exactly what is being asked of you and what the project involves before you answer.

- Review your schedule to see if you really have the time to do a quality job. ("If you have to have an answer immediately, it is 'no.' If you can wait a few days for me to finish project X, and review my schedule, I'll take a careful look at it.")

Figure 9.2 Time Management Types

Type	Explanation	Do You Have Any of These Tendencies?	What Actions Make You Like This Type of Person?	What Can You Do to Begin Eliminating This Type of Behavior?
The Circler	Doing the same things over and over again and again and hoping for a different result; basically, going around in circles.	YES NO		
The Doodler	Not paying attention to details, doing things that do not really matter to the completion of your project.	YES NO		
The Squanderer	Wasting too much time trying to "get ready" to work and never really getting anything done until it is too late to do a good job.	YES NO		
The Beggar	Expecting time to stop for you after you've wasted time doing nothing or going in circles, then becoming frustrated when you don't have enough time.	YES NO		
The Planner	Planning out your project so carefully and meticulously that by the time you have everything you think you need, there is no time to really do the project.	YES NO		
The Hun	Waiting too late to plan or get things done and then stomping on anyone or anything to get the project done with no regard for others' feelings, time, or relationships.	YES NO		
The Passivist	Convincing yourself that you'll never get it all done and that there is no use to try anyway.	YES NO		

How can becoming a more organized person help you manage your time more effectively?

Shutterstock

- Learn the difference between assertiveness (politely declining) and rudeness ("Have you lost your mind?").

- Learn how to put yourself and your future first (for a change). By doing this, you can say "yes" more often later on.

- Inform others of your time management schedule so that they will have a better understanding of why you say "no."

- If you must say "yes" to an unwanted project (something at work, for example), try to negotiate a deadline that works for everyone—you first!

- Keep your "no" short. If you have to offer an explanation, be brief so that you don't talk yourself into doing something you can't do and to avoid giving false hope to the other person. If the answer is "no" right now and it will be "no" in the future, say so now. Don't smile, because that indicates "maybe."

- If you feel you simply have to say "yes," try to trade off with the other person and ask him or her to do something on your list.

- Put a time limit on your "yes." For example, you might agree to help someone but you could say, "I can give you 30 minutes and then I have to leave."

BEGINNING YOUR DAY WITH PEACE

Can You Start Your Day as a Blank Page and Simplify Your Life?

Imagine a day with nothing to do! That may be difficult, if not impossible, for you to conceive right now. But as an exercise in building your own day from scratch and simplifying your life, think about having a day where you build your schedule and where you do not have to be constrained by activities and projects that others have thrust on you. Think about a day where you are in charge. Crazy? Impossible? Outrageous? Maybe not as much as you think.

Yes, you will need to plot activities such as work, training, and family duties into your daily calendar, but you also need to learn how to schedule time for fun activities, time for silence and peace, and time to be alone with your thoughts. By learning how to build your schedule each evening from scratch, you have the opportunity to plan a day where you simplify your life. There is an old quote that states, "If you want to know what you value in your life, look at your checkbook and your calendar." Basically, this suggests that we spend our money and time on things we value.

12 Ways to Simplify Your Life

- Know what you value and work hard to eliminate activities that are not in conjunction with your core value system. This can be whittled down to one statement: "Identify what is important to you. Eliminate everything else." Match your priorities with your goals and values.

- Get away from technology for a few hours a day. Turn off your computer, cell phone, iPod, and other devices that can take time from what you value.

- Learn to delegate. You may say to yourself, "My family does not know how to use the washing machine." Guess what? When all of their underwear is dirty, they'll learn how to use it. Don't enable others to avoid activities that complicate your life.

- Make a list of everything you are doing. Prioritize this list into what you enjoy doing and what fits into your value system. If you can only feasibly do three or four of these activities per day, draw a line after number four and eliminate the rest of the list.

- Do what is essential for the well-being of you and your family and eliminate everything else. Delegate some things to family members of all ages that they can accomplish. Don't waste time saving money. This doesn't mean not to save money—it means not to be "penny wise and pound foolish." Spend money to save time. In other words, don't drive across town to save three cents per gallon on fuel or 10 cents for a gallon of milk. Pay the extra money and have more time to do what you like.

- Clean your home of clutter and mess. Make sure everything has a place. Do the same thing at work. Get rid of things you don't need.

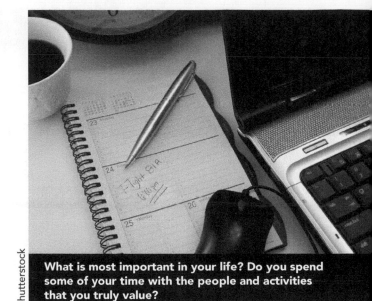

What is most important in your life? Do you spend some of your time with the people and activities that you truly value?

- Donate everything you don't need or use to charity. Simplifying your life may also mean simplifying your closets, drawers, cabinets, and garage. If we are not careful, we are soon possessed by our possessions.

- Go through your home or apartment and eliminate everything that does not bring you joy or have sentimental value. If you don't love it or need it or use it, ditch it.

- Clean up the files on your computer. Erase everything that you don't need or want so that you can find material more easily. If you have not used the file in a month, put it on a flash drive for later use.

- Live in the moment. Yes, it is important to plan for the future, but if you ignore "the moment," your future will not be as bright. Although it is important to plan for the future, it is equally important to live today!

- Spend a few moments each morning and afternoon reflecting on all of the abundance in your life. Learn to give thanks and learn to do nothing. Count your blessings. (Adapted from Zen Habits, 2008; and Baca, 2009)

In Figure 9.3, compile a list that can help you simplify your life in each category. Add only those things to the list that you can actually do on a daily basis.

THE DREADED "P" WORD

Why Is Procrastination So Easy to Do and How Can You Beat It Once and for All?

It's not just you! Almost all of us procrastinate, and then we worry and tell ourselves, "I'll never do it again if I can just get through this one project." We say things to ourselves like, "If I can just live through this project, I will never wait until the last minute again." But someone comes along with a great idea for fun, and off we go. Or there is a great movie on TV, the kids want to play a game of ball, you go to the refrigerator for snack, and before you know it, you reward yourself with free time before you have done your work. You have to work first; then reward yourself with play.

> If you have to eat two frogs, eat the ugliest one first.
> —Brian Tracy

The truth is simple: We tend to avoid the hard jobs in favor of the easy ones. Even many of the list makers fool themselves. They mark off a long list of easy tasks while the big ones still loom in front of them. Many of us put off unpleasant tasks until our back is against the

Figure 9.3 Ways to Simplify Your Life

Two things I can do to simplify my life at home	
Two things I can do to simplify my life at work	
Two things I can do to simplify my life with technology (using cell phones, texting, etc.)	
Two things I can do to simplify my life with my children, friends, or pets	
Two things I can do to simplify my life with my spouse/partner/loved one	
Two things I can do to simplify my financial matters	

> Don't wait. The time will never be just right.
> —Napoleon Hill

POSITIVE HABITS at Work

Make it a habit never to go home from work until you have made your to do list for the next day. Although you may be tired, you will be able to begin work immediately the next morning, and this will put you way ahead of the average employee, who leaves without thinking about the next day. Being prepared and organized is also a great stress reliever.

wall. So why do we procrastinate when we all know how unpleasant the results can be? Why aren't we disciplined, organized, and controlled so we can reap the rewards that come from being prepared? Why do we put ourselves through so much stress just by putting things off?

The biggest problem with procrastination, even beyond not getting the job, task, or paper completed, is *doing it poorly* and then suffering the stress caused by putting it off and not doing our best work. By putting the project off, you have cheated yourself of the time needed to bring your best to the table. Most likely, you are going to hand over a project, *with your name on it,* that is not even close to your potential. If you know your work is not good, so will your boss and your colleagues.

What has procrastination cost you? This is perhaps one of the most important questions that you can answer with regard to managing your time more effectively. Did it cost you an opportunity to look good in the eyes of your boss? Did it cost you money? Did it cost you your reputation? Did it cost you your dignity? Did it cost you your ability to do your best? Did it cost you a friend? ***Procrastination is not free.*** Every time you do it, it costs you something. You need to determine what it is worth.

In order to beat procrastination, you will also need to consider ***what type*** of procrastinator you are. Each type requires a different strategy and different energy to overcome, but make no mistake about it, success requires overcoming all degrees and types of procrastination. Which are you? Consider Figure 9.4.

Take a moment and complete the Time Management Assessment in Figure 9.5. Be honest and truthful with your responses. The results of your score are located after the assessment.

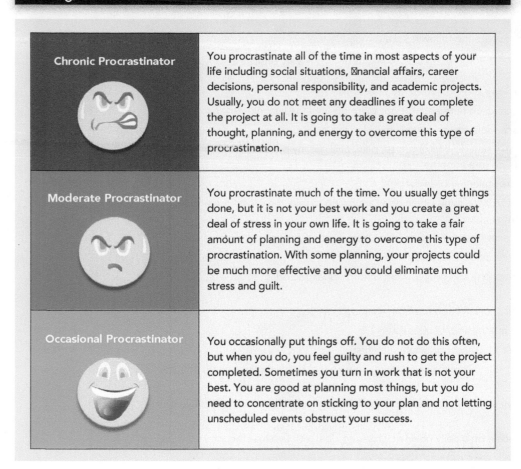

Figure 9.4 Procrastinator Types

Chronic Procrastinator	You procrastinate all of the time in most aspects of your life including social situations, financial affairs, career decisions, personal responsibility, and academic projects. Usually, you do not meet any deadlines if you complete the project at all. It is going to take a great deal of thought, planning, and energy to overcome this type of procrastination.
Moderate Procrastinator	You procrastinate much of the time. You usually get things done, but it is not your best work and you create a great deal of stress in your own life. It is going to take a fair amount of planning and energy to overcome this type of procrastination. With some planning, your projects could be much more effective and you could eliminate much stress and guilt.
Occasional Procrastinator	You occasionally put things off. You do not do this often, but when you do, you feel guilty and rush to get the project completed. Sometimes you turn in work that is not your best. You are good at planning most things, but you do need to concentrate on sticking to your plan and not letting unscheduled events obstruct your success.

GETTING THE MOST OUT OF THIS MOMENT

Do You Know the Causes of and Cures for Procrastination?

Below, you will find a list of the 10 most common causes of procrastination and some simple, doable, everyday strategies that you can employ to overcome each cause.

Superhuman Expectations and Trying to Be a Perfectionist

- Allow yourself more time than you think you need to complete a project.
- Allow enough time to do your very best and let that be that. If you plan and allow time for excellence, you can't do more.

Fear of Not Knowing How to Do the Task

- Ask for clarification from whomever asked you to do the project.
- Read as much as you can about the task at hand and ask for help.
- Break up big tasks into small ones.

Figure 9.5 Time Management Assessment

Answer the following questions with the following scale:

1 = Not at all   2 = Rarely   3 = Sometimes   4 = Often   5 = Very often

1. I prioritize my tasks every day and work from my priority list.		1 2 3 4 5
2. I work hard to complete tasks on time and not put them off until the last minute.		1 2 3 4 5
3. I take time to plan and schedule the next day's activities the night before.		1 2 3 4 5
4. I make time during my daily schedule to organize, plan, and get my projects completed so that I can have more quality time at home.		1 2 3 4 5
5. I get my work done before I take fun breaks.		1 2 3 4 5
6. I analyze my assignments to determine which ones are going to take the most time and then work on them first and most often.		1 2 3 4 5
7. I have analyzed my daily activities and determined where I actually spend my time.		1 2 3 4 5
8. I know how to say "no" and do so frequently.		1 2 3 4 5
9. I know how to avoid distractions and how to work through unexpected interruptions. 1 2 3 4 5		
10. I do not let "fear of the unknown" keep me from working on a project.		1 2 3 4 5
11. I know how to overcome apathy and/or laziness.		1 2 3 4 5
12. I always tackle the difficult and most important jobs first.		1 2 3 4 5
13. I know how to reframe a project that may not interest me so that I can see the benefit in it and learn from it.		1 2 3 4 5
14. I know how to break down a major, complex, or overwhelming task to get it done in pieces and then put it all together.		1 2 3 4 5
15. I build time into my schedule on a daily or weekly basis to deal with unexpected interruptions or distractions.		1 2 3 4 5

YOUR TOTAL SCORE: _____

RESULTS:

60–75 You manage your time well and you know how to build a schedule to get things done. Your productivity is high. You don't let procrastination rule your life.

45–59 You are good at doing some things on time, but you tend to procrastinate too much. Learning how to build and work from a priority list may help you manage your time more effectively.

30–44 You need to work hard to change your time management skills and learn how to set realistic goals. Procrastination is probably a major issue for you, causing you much stress and worry. Working from a priority list can help you greatly.

29–below Your time management skills are very weak and without improvement, your career could be in jeopardy. You could benefit from learning to set realistic goals, working from a priority list, and reframing your thought process toward tasks.

Lack of Motivation

- Reframe your attitude to find the benefit in any task.
- Consider how this task will help you reach your overall goals and dreams.
- Take time to do the things you love, creating a healthy balance in your life.

Fear of Failing or Fear of the Task Being Too Hard

- Start the project with positive, optimistic thoughts.
- Face your fears; look them right in the face and make a decision to defeat them.
- Visualize your successful completion of the project.

No Real Plan or Goal for Getting the Task Done

- Set reasonable, concrete goals that you can reach in about 20 to 25 minutes.
- Draw up an action plan the night before you begin the project.
- Look at completing the project in terms of your long-range goals and your overall life plan.

Considering the Task Too Unpleasant or Uninteresting

- Realize that most tasks are not as unpleasant as we've made them out to be.
- Do the hardest tasks first, and save the easiest for last.
- Schedule tasks that you consider unpleasant to be done during your peak hours.

Laziness and/or Apathy

- Concentrate on the rewards of managing yourself and your time more effectively.
- Give yourself a time limit to accomplish a task.

Distractions and/or Lack of Focus

- Close your door and make yourself get started. Turn your desk away from the door, and people are less likely to interrupt you.
- Start on the difficult, most boring tasks first.
- Weed out your personal belongings and living space. Organization helps you manage your time and get to work.

Choosing Fun Before Responsibility

- Reward yourself when you have accomplished an important body of work.
- Don't get involved in too many organizations, accept too many commitments, or overextend yourself. Allow enough time to concentrate on what needs to be done.
- Consider the consequences of not doing what you're responsible for doing.

Waiting for the "Right" Mood

- Avoid whining and complaining, and realize that the right mood can be created by you at any time.
- Just do it! Force yourself to jump into the task.
- Work during your peak hours of the day.

EVALUATING HOW YOU SPEND YOUR TIME

Do You Know Where Your Time Goes?

So how do you find out where your time goes? The same way that you find out where your money goes—you track it. Every 15 minutes for one week, you will record exactly how you spent that time. This exercise may seem a little tedious at first, but if you will complete the process over a period of a week, you will have a much better concept of where your time is being used. Yes, that's right—for a week, you need to keep a written record of how much time you spend sleeping, reading, eating, working, getting to class and back, cooking, caring for children, walking pets, watching television, doing yard work, going to movies, attending athletic events, hanging out, doing laundry, whatever. You will probably be surprised at where your time really goes.

Take your plan with you and keep track of your activities during the day. To make things simple, round off tasks to 15-minute intervals. For example, if you start walking to the cafeteria at 7:08, you might want to mark off the time block that begins with 7:00. If you finish eating

GRADUATE *Quote*

Christian Garcia
Graduate!
UEI College, Ontario, CA
Career: Associate Director of Education,
UEI College

My advice to anyone in college would be to love what you do. If you truly love what you do, then the old quote is true: "You'll never have to work a day in your life." This is how I feel every day. I actually tell my friends that I stopped working in 1999 because I found my joy—my passion. I would also say that you have to seek opportunities because they usually do not come to you; you have to go to them.

and return to your home at 7:49, you can mark off the next two blocks. You will also want to note the activity so you can evaluate how you spent your time later. Study the example that is provided for you in Figure 9.6.

In Figure 9.7 you will find a daily time log for you to use for this exercise. Remember to take these pages with you and record how you are spending your time during the day. As you progress through the week, try to improve the use of your time. When you finish this exercise, review how you spent your time.

Figure 9.6   How You Really Spend Your Time

7:00	get up & shower	7:00		12:15
	✕	7:15		12:30
		7:30	Walked to Union	12:45
	Breakfast	7:45	1:00 Ate lunch	1:00
8:00		8:00		1:15
		8:15		1:30
	Read paper	8:30	Talked w/ Joe	1:45
	Walked to class	8:45	2:00	2:00
9:00	English 101	9:00	Went to book	2:15
		9:15	store	2:30
		9:30	Walked to	2:45
		9:45	3:00 my room	3:00
10:00		10:00	Called Ron	3:15
		10:15		3:30
		10:30		3:45
	Walked to class	10:45	4:00 Watched	4:00
11:00	History 210	11:00	TV	4:15
		11:15		4:30
		11:30	Walked to	4:45
		11:45	5:00 library	5:00
12:00		12:00		5:15

Figure 9.7 Daily Time Sheet

Monday		Tuesday		Wednesday	
6:00	6:00	6:00	6:00	6:00	6:00
	6:15		6:15		6:15
	6:30		6:30		6:30
	6:45		6:45		6:45
7:00	7:00	7:00	7:00	7:00	7:00
	7:15		7:15		7:15
	7:30		7:30		7:30
	7:45		7:45		7:45
8:00	8:00	8:00	8:00	8:00	8:00
	8:15		8:15		8:15
	8:30		8:30		8:30
	8:45		8:45		8:45
9:00	9:00	9:00	9:00	9:00	9:00
	9:15		9:15		9:15
	9:30		9:30		9:30
	9:45		9:45		9:45
10:00	10:00	10:00	10:00	10:00	10:00
	10:15		10:15		10:15
	10:30		10:30		10:30
	10:45		10:45		10:45
11:00	11:00	11:00	11:00	11:00	11:00
	11:15		11:15		11:15
	11:30		11:30		11:30
	11:45		11:45		11:45
12:00	12:00	12:00	12:00	12:00	12:00
	12:15		12:15		12:15
	12:30		12:30		12:30
	12:45		12:45		12:45
1:00	1:00	1:00	1:00	1:00	1:00
	1:15		1:15		1:15
	1:30		1:30		1:30
	1:45		1:45		1:45
2:00	2:00	2:00	2:00	2:00	2:00
	2:15		2:15		2:15
	2:30		2:30		2:30
	2:45		2:45		2:45
3:00	3:00	3:00	3:00	3:00	3:00
	3:15		3:15		3:15
	3:30		3:30		3:30
	3:45		3:45		3:45
4:00	4:00	4:00	4:00	4:00	4:00
	4:15		4:15		4:15
	4:30		4:30		4:30
	4:45		4:45		4:45
5:00	5:00	5:00	5:00	5:00	5:00
	5:15		5:15		5:15
	5:30		5:30		5:30
	5:45		5:45		5:45
6:00	6:00	6:00	6:00	6:00	6:00
	6:15		6:15		6:15
	6:30		6:30		6:30
	6:45		6:45		6:45
7:00	7:00	7:00	7:00	7:00	7:00
	7:15		7:15		7:15
	7:30		7:30		7:30
	7:45		7:45		7:45
8:00	8:00	8:00	8:00	8:00	8:00
	8:15		8:15		8:15
	8:30		8:30		8:30
	8:45		8:45		8:45
9:00	9:00	9:00	9:00	9:00	9:00
	9:15		9:15		9:15
	9:30		9:30		9:30
	9:45		9:45		9:45
10:00	10:00	10:00	10:00	10:00	10:00
	10:15		10:15		10:15
	10:30		10:30		10:30
	10:45		10:45		10:45
11:00	11:00	11:00	11:00	11:00	11:00
	11:15		11:15		11:15
	11:30		11:30		11:30
	11:45		11:45		11:45
12:00	12:00	12:00	12:00	12:00	12:00

(continued)

Figure 9.7 Daily Time Sheet (continued)

Thursday		Friday		Saturday		Sunday	
6:00	6:00	6:00	6:00	6:00	6:00	6:00	6:00
	6:15		6:15		6:15		6:15
	6:30		6:30		6:30		6:30
	6:45		6:45		6:45		6:45
7:00	7:00	7:00	7:00	7:00	7:00	7:00	7:00
	7:15		7:15		7:15		7:15
	7:30		7:30		7:30		7:30
	7:45		7:45		7:45		7:45
8:00	8:00	8:00	8:00	8:00	8:00	8:00	8:00
	8:15		8:15		8:15		8:15
	8:30		8:30		8:30		8:30
	8:45		8:45		8:45		8:45
9:00	9:00	9:00	9:00	9:00	9:00	9:00	9:00
	9:15		9:15		9:15		9:15
	9:30		9:30		9:30		9:30
	9:45		9:45		9:45		9:45
10:00	10:00	10:00	10:00	10:00	10:00	10:00	10:00
	10:15		10:15		10:15		10:15
	10:30		10:30		10:30		10:30
	10:45		10:45		10:45		10:45
11:00	11:00	11:00	11:00	11:00	11:00	11:00	11:00
	11:15		11:15		11:15		11:15
	11:30		11:30		11:30		11:30
	11:45		11:45		11:45		11:45
12:00	12:00	12:00	12:00	12:00	12:00	12:00	12:00
	12:15		12:15		12:15		12:15
	12:30		12:30		12:30		12:30
	12:45		12:45		12:45		12:45
1:00	1:00	1:00	1:00	1:00	1:00	1:00	1:00
	1:15		1:15		1:15		1:15
	1:30		1:30		1:30		1:30
	1:45		1:45		1:45		1:45
2:00	2:00	2:00	2:00	2:00	2:00	2:00	2:00
	2:15		2:15		2:15		2:15
	2:30		2:30		2:30		2:30
	2:45		2:45		2:45		2:45
3:00	3:00	3:00	3:00	3:00	3:00	3:00	3:00
	3:15		3:15		3:15		3:15
	3:30		3:30		3:30		3:30
	3:45		3:45		3:45		3:45
4:00	4:00	4:00	4:00	4:00	4:00	4:00	4:00
	4:15		4:15		4:15		4:15
	4:30		4:30		4:30		4:30
	4:45		4:45		4:45		4:45
5:00	5:00	5:00	5:00	5:00	5:00	5:00	5:00
	5:15		5:15		5:15		5:15
	5:30		5:30		5:30		5:30
	5:45		5:45		5:45		5:45
6:00	6:00	6:00	6:00	6:00	6:00	6:00	6:00
	6:15		6:15		6:15		6:15
	6:30		6:30		6:30		6:30
	6:45		6:45		6:45		6:45
7:00	7:00	7:00	7:00	7:00	7:00	7:00	7:00
	7:15		7:15		7:15		7:15
	7:30		7:30		7:30		7:30
	7:45		7:45		7:45		7:45
8:00	8:00	8:00	8:00	8:00	8:00	8:00	8:00
	8:15		8:15		8:15		8:15
	8:30		8:30		8:30		8:30
	8:45		8:45		8:45		8:45
9:00	9:00	9:00	9:00	9:00	9:00	9:00	9:00
	9:15		9:15		9:15		9:15
	9:30		9:30		9:30		9:30
	9:45		9:45		9:45		9:45
10:00	10:00	10:00	10:00	10:00	10:00	10:00	10:00
	10:15		10:15		10:15		10:15
	10:30		10:30		10:30		10:30
	10:45		10:45		10:45		10:45
11:00	11:00	11:00	11:00	11:00	11:00	11:00	11:00
	11:15		11:15		11:15		11:15
	11:30		11:30		11:30		11:30
	11:45		11:45		11:45		11:45
12:00	12:00	12:00	12:00	12:00	12:00	12:00	12:00

ELIMINATING DISTRACTIONS AND INTERRUPTIONS

When Is Enough Really Enough?

If you were diligent and kept an accurate account of all of your time, your evaluation will probably reveal that much of your time is spent dealing with distractions, getting side-tracked, and handling interruptions. These three things account for much of the time wasted within a 24-hour period. In Figure 9.8, you will find a list of some of the most common distractions faced

Figure 9.8 Common Distractions

Common Distractions	My Plan to Overcome These Distractions
Friends/family dropping by unexpectedly at home	
Colleagues stopping by your work space and talking when you are trying to work	
Working on small, unimportant tasks while the big, career-changing jobs go undone or get done poorly	
Spending too much time on breaks and at lunch when you should be working	
Taking time to read mindless e-mails and jokes sent by people who have nothing else to do	
Technology (playing on YouTube, Facebook, iTunes, Google, etc.)	
Constant phone calls that do not pertain to anything of importance	
Not setting aside any time during the day to deal with the unexpected	
Friends/family demanding things of you because they do not understand your schedule or commitments	
Not blocking private time in your daily schedule	
Being disorganized and spending hours piddling and calling it "work"	
Playing with your children or pets before your tasks are complete (and not scheduling time to be with them in the first place)	
Saying "yes" when you need to say "no"	
Other distractions faced by you	

by people who are pursuing a career. Consider how you might deal with these distractions in an effective, assertive manner.

PLANNING AND PREPARING

Is There a Secret to Time Management?

In the past, you may have said to yourself, "I don't have time to plan." "I don't like to be fenced in and tied to a rigid schedule." "I have so many duties that planning never works." Scheduling does not have to be a tedious chore or something you dread. Scheduling can be your lifeline to more free time. After all, if you build your own schedule, it is yours! As much as you are able, build your schedule the way you want and need it.

To manage your time successfully, you need to spend some time planning. To plan successfully, you need a calendar that has a week-at-a-glance or month-at-a-glance section as well as sections for daily notes and appointments. Most companies will furnish a calendar, but it they don't, you can download one from the Internet or create one using Word or another computer program.

Planning and Organizing for Work

Each evening, you should take a few minutes (and literally, that is all it will take) and sit in a quiet place and make a list of all that needs to be done tomorrow. Successful time management comes from **planning the night before!** Let's say your list looks like the one in Figure 9.9.

Next, separate this list into three categories, as shown in Figure 9.10.

Don't get too excited yet. Your time management plan is ***not finished.*** The most important part is still ahead of you. Now, you will need to rank the items in order of their importance. You will put a 1 by the most important tasks, a 2 by the next most important tasks, and so on in each category, as shown in Figure 9.11.

You have now created a plan to actually get these tasks done! Not only have you created your list, but now you have divided the tasks into important categories, ranked them, and made a written commitment to them.

Figure 9.9 To Do List

To Do List	
Research procurement project	Exercise
Write report for supervisor— due next week	Go to movie
	Buy birthday card for Mom
Prepare for next training class two days from now	Wash the car
	Take shirts to dry cleaner
Schedule team mtg. at work	Buy groceries
Attend department meeting at 8:00 a.m.	Call Janice about weekend
Meet with supervisor at 10:00 a.m.	

Figure 9.10 — Setting Priorities for To Do List

Must Do	Need to Do	Would Like to Do
Prepare for training class	Research procurement project	Wash the car
Exercise	Buy birthday card for Mom	Call Janice about weekend
Schedule team meeting at work	Take shirts to cleaner	Go to movie
Department meeting at 8:00 a.m.	Buy groceries	
Meeting with supervisor at 10:00 a.m.	Write report for supervisor	

Figure 9.11 — Ranking Priorities for To Do List

Must Do	Need to Do	Would Like to Do
4 Prepare for training class	1 Research procurement project	3 Wash the car
5 Exercise	5 Buy birthday card for Mom	1 Call Janice about weekend
3 Schedule team meeting at work	4 Take shirts to cleaner	2 Go to movie
1 Department meeting at 8:00 a.m.	3 Buy groceries	
2 Meeting with supervisor at 10:00 a.m.	2 Write report for supervisor	

If these were real tasks, you would now schedule them into your daily calendar (see Figure 9.12). You would schedule category 1 (MUST DO) first, category 2 (NEED TO DO) next, and category 3 (WOULD LIKE TO DO) last. Remember, never keep more than one calendar. Always carry it with you and always schedule your tasks immediately so that you won't forget them.

Great Tips for New Employees

Good time management often boils down to doing a few things extremely well and doing them over and over. When you go to work, the big things count—but so do the little ones! If you have a family, you will need to be highly organized so you can spend quality time with them.

- Break up big jobs into little ones so they don't overwhelm you.
- Allow yourself enough time to complete a task with a few extra minutes, in case there is a glitch. Work expands to fill up whatever amount of time you have, so push yourself to complete the job in a reasonable time frame.

Figure 9.12 Daily Calendar

DAY	Monday	Priority	Complete?
Time	**Task**		
6:00			Yes No
6:30			Yes No
7:00	Study for finance		Yes No
7:30	↓		Yes No
8:00	English 101		Yes No
8:30			Yes No
9:00	↓		Yes No
9:30	Read Pg. 1–10 of Chem. Chapter		Yes No
10:00	Management 210		Yes No
10:30			Yes No
11:00	↓		Yes No
11:30	Finish Reading Chem. Chapter		Yes No
12:00			Yes No
12:30	↓		Yes No
1:00	Meet w/Chemistry group (take lunch)		Yes No
1:30	↓		Yes No
2:00	Work		Yes No
2:30			Yes No
3:00			Yes No
3:30			Yes No
4:00			Yes No
4:30			Yes No
5:00			Yes No
5:30			Yes No
6:00	↓		Yes No
6:30	Dinner/run by grocery store		Yes No
7:00	↓		Yes No
7:30	Internet Research for speech		Yes No
8:00			Yes No
8:30	↓		Yes No
9:00	call Janice @ w/end		Yes No
9:30			Yes No

- If you are still taking courses or working on another degree, set up a regular time to study and stick to it.
- When you have a project, set reasonable goals that you can meet in 20- to 25-minute blocks.
- Take short breaks; get up from your computer and move around. Leave your desk for lunch and breaks; you'll come back refreshed. Don't ever eat lunch at your desk unless you have to.
- Allow yourself longer than you think you need for a project so you don't have to stay up all night.
- Avoid having to cram for school or work projects by starting early.
- Don't get too involved with outside organizations and commitments that steal your time and make you look slack at work.

- Start on the most difficult, boring jobs first. Reward yourself with something you enjoy after you have completed a good block of work.

- Weed out personal belongings; get rid of clutter that takes your time. Streamline your house, your workspace, your home desk, and your garage.

- File things as you go; don't pile them in stacks. Don't allow yourself to be one of those people who would rather "pile than file," because you will never be able to find important documents.

- If you have children, give each one a workspace with his or her own supplies. Give each child a file drawer or box to keep important papers that he or she will need again. You are teaching your children time management and organization skills.

- Handle paperwork immediately and only once.

- Organize your workspace and designate a specific place for your supplies. Keep supplies on hand so you don't run out at a crucial time.

- Prepare to be successful at work or school by getting ready the evening before. Decide what you are going to wear; press your clothes if they need it; polish your shoes.

- Keep a Rolodex file, iPod, or other system for important phone numbers and addresses you use frequently.

- Organize as effectively at home as you do at work.

- Plan a rotation schedule for housework. Clean one room each day.

- Organize your closets and dresser drawers, ridding yourself of clutter and things you don't use anymore.

- Fill up your gas tank the night before to avoid stress in the morning.

- If you are a perfectionist, get over it! Some things need to be perfect, but most don't.

- Take time to do things you love and create a healthy balance in your life. If you reward the completion of a big job by immediately beginning another big job, you have a good chance of becoming a workaholic.

- If you have children, schedule at least one hour a week with each one. Make this a happy, special time. Sunday nights are great for family night.

- Make family meals happy. Sit down together at least three times a week. Let the children help prepare the meal and set the table. Allow each person to tell about his or her day.

- Put fun days on your calendar and keep them sacred.

- Put family days on your calendar and have everyone help get things done so you can have a great family event.

NAVIGATING LAND MINES

How Do I Avoid Problems from Day One?

From the first day on, it is very important to perform your duties in an outstanding manner and convince your bosses that they made a good decision in hiring you. You should perform at your highest level every day and be willing to learn. Sometimes this means being willing to do the "dirty work" that no one else wants to do. It might mean arriving early and staying late at times. It will almost certainly mean that you will be sitting in classes or studying some phase of company regulations in front of a computer screen as you become oriented to the company.

In some cases, you will be on probation for a certain period of time, usually 90 days, so it is imperative that you perform at the top of your game during this time. The majority of companies conduct regular, formal performance appraisals. Ask for a copy of the evaluation instrument, study the items on which you will be evaluated, and be sure you are performing all of them at a high level. You don't want any surprises when the boss evaluates you. It is not unusual for employees to think they are doing what is expected of them only to learn at evaluation time that they have missed the mark. Although doing your job well is key, it is also important to be looking toward a promotion and your next career opportunity. Observe people in leadership roles who have done well and are respected by their colleagues: What is their educational background? How do they communicate? What do they do that sets them apart? Study the trends in your industry. Read good books, business journals, and trade journals in your field. What can you learn from books and journals that you can apply to your own work and perhaps do a better, more creative job?

"WATER COOLER" GOSSIP GROUPS

How Much Can a Little Gossip Hurt?

There are very few people who don't like to gossip. The workplace is no exception to this rule. Rumors fly around all the time, many of which have no real substance whatsoever; in fact, some people love to take a little tidbit of information and embellish it until there is no truth whatsoever. The problem with this little exercise is that it hurts the people who are the subjects of this unfounded gossip. The other problem is that everybody knows who the rumormongers are, and nobody trusts them. It's not hard to tell who goes up and down the halls spreading malicious gossip. A sure way to damage your personal reputation is to become one of these people. A good thing to remember is that stepping on one's feelings is as painful as stepping on one's toes, and it lasts a lot longer.

Never Speak Negatively about Your Boss or Former Employer

Think about this quote: "If you work for a man, work for him, or find another job." This is good advice whether your boss is a man or woman! While it is absolutely certain that some bosses won't earn your respect or deserve your loyalty, he or she is the boss nevertheless. Not every boss is a good supervisor, but he or she is still the boss. You will be very fortunate if you get a boss who is visionary, fair, honest, ethical, and caring, and who tries to help all employees grow and to learn. Even if you have a lousy boss, if you are going to take the paycheck, you need to give a good day's work for a good day's pay.

Many bosses will tell you that the number one quality they value is loyalty. This doesn't mean that you can't disagree with the boss. It just means that you disagree with him or her in person and that you do it respectfully. Should you choose to disagree with your boss, you need to choose your words carefully and say something like this: "Mrs. Brown, I know you have so much more experience than I do, and I may be way off base, but it seems to me that the decision to close that branch might be a little premature. Are you aware that XYZ company is getting ready to build a big plant within half a mile of that branch?"

Never make the boss look bad in front of anyone to show how smart and clever you are. If you have a boss who truly encourages speaking up and disagreeing in meetings—and these are rare—be sure that even then you use a respectful tone of voice and that you don't say or do anything that causes the boss to lose face. No one—including a boss—ever forgets being embarrassed in front of his or her colleagues.

Figure out what is near and dear to the boss's heart and work hard to make it happen. This is not being underhanded; it's just using good sense. Don't let your boss hear bad news from someone else if you know about it. Bosses don't like surprises. They especially don't like to hear about it from their own bosses.

When you go for an interview, never say anything bad about the company or your present or former boss. Even if he or she deserves to be attacked, the person interviewing you will assume that you will be negative when you go to work with the new company, and most likely, you won't get the job offer.

Paying Attention to Workplace Politics

Politics is rampant in the workplace! You will see "kissing up," "brown-nosing," lying, bullying, exaggerating, people taking credit for others' work—the list goes on and on. The secret is to know what is going on without being a participant in the negative aspects of office politics. Most people know which colleagues are spreading the rumors, attacking others, playing up to the boss, and so on. You can't stop politics, so don't waste your time trying.

The only way you can avoid politics is to go to work in the middle of a forest and never see anyone else. The good news is that not all politics are bad. You don't have to change who you are to be successful at office politics. Nice guys do finish first most of the time. J. W. Marriott, CEO of Marriott Corporation, said, "The closer you get to the top, the nicer people are." You can be thoughtful, sincere, considerate, and interested in others, and your chances of succeeding are far better than those who choose to use dirty politics.

Some people believe that office politics are only played by people who can't get ahead by any other means, but according to Herminia Ibarra, associate professor at Harvard Business School, "You don't have to be a jerk to make things happen. Integrity can be a source of power." Lou DiNatale, senior fellow at the McCormick Institute of Public Affairs at the University of Massachusetts, says, "Real political power is about pulling other people to your ideas, and then pushing those ideas through to other people." Today it seems that people value knowledge and skills far more than they do negative politics. Politics will only take you so far, and if your power is attached to someone else's, when he or she falls from grace, so will you, especially if you have been a backstabber to other people.

There will always be a grapevine. It has been said that 80 percent of what comes down the grapevine is true. If you are the boss, you need to put the truth down the grapevine as often as you can. If you hear a rumor and you know it is not true, simply say, "That's not true. I was in that meeting, and Mr. Carter didn't say that. This is what he said."

Politics will always exist. Know what is going on around you at all times, but refuse to be a player in underhanded, dirty politics. Practice honesty, integrity, fairness, and decency, and if you are good at your job, you will succeed. Take time to get to know people on a personal level; don't judge them based on what anyone else says. Just because one person has a problem with a colleague doesn't mean you have to.

What does this statement mean?

Never judge another person through someone else's eyes.

Avoid Backstabbing and Trampling on Others

There are many ways to trample on others' feelings, and you will probably encounter or observe most of them. The important thing is for you to avoid participating in such behavior. Some of the typical behaviors that people hate most are:

- Having someone take credit for their work
- Colleagues who don't perform their work well and on time so someone else falls behind and looks bad
- Unfounded rumors, such as untrue accusations about having an affair
- Schmoozing those at the top and scorning those below them
- Spreading rumors about people to cause animosity with the idea that the gossiper will come out on top
- Resisting requests for information that a person needs to do his or her job
- Bullying by loud, intimidating colleagues
- Laughter at some off-color or inappropriate joke that hurts another colleague
- Being left out of the loop intentionally on things that should be common knowledge

> *One in five employees reports being bullied at work.*
> —Valerie Cade, *Bullyfree Workplace*

Just as these behaviors hurt you, they also hurt other employees. You will be respected if you refuse to participate in these games. If someone mistreats you, gather your courage, go to his or her office, and say something like, "I was told that you were spreading a rumor about me that isn't true, so I decided to ask you if you did this. Did you say I was having an affair with Mr. Kendall?" Since most people who trample on others and backstab their colleagues are chickens underneath their loud exteriors, the person will probably deny having said it and probably won't say it again. You can respond, "Well, I didn't think you were that kind of person, and I'm glad to know you aren't doing such a despicable thing. So we don't have a problem." The chances are good that this person will not target you again.

WORKPLACE ROMANCES

What's Love Got to Do with It?

Is it something in the air? Or is it the music that plays constantly in many offices? Or is it the close proximity of office cubicles? No one seems to know what causes so many office romances, but "almost half of us have been romantically tied to someone from work, and many more would like to find amour in a neighboring cubicle" (Vault.com, 2010). Office romances seem to be rather common today. After all, employees spend up to one-third of their time at work in close quarters with other people. While office romances are not as taboo as they once were, for best results, cupid is best left out of the office.

What does your company's policy say about office relationships? Read this as soon as possible, before an office romance is even remotely possible. Before you jump into a romantic relationship with a coworker, you really need to think about it carefully. This may seem like the love of your life, the soulmate you have longed for. But what happens if this romance goes sour? What have you got to lose if it doesn't work out? Or even if it does work out?

In a worst-case scenario, you could lose your job. Some companies' corporate regulations forbid romantic relationships. You could damage your professional reputation, and in some cases, even be charged for sexual harassment if you get your life tangled up with the wrong person. Certainly, you know by now that everyone is not honest and ethical, much less responsible. If you have a relationship that doesn't work out, naturally, it would be much easier if this took place somewhere besides your office.

According to Joni Johnston, president and CEO of WorkRelationships.com, "Most dating relationships end. Think of the number of people we date and the number we end up marrying—the odds are not good." Is this relationship worth the gossip that will surely go on around you? (Remember, there are very few secrets at work.) Could you become involved in some kind of jealous triangle? Are the quarters too close for comfort to keep an office romance going? You have always heard the old expression, "Look before you leap." This is one of those times when you really need to weigh all the consequences before jumping in and getting in way over your head.

All that said, and even if it is not a good idea, it is virtually impossible to stop love from happening. Because you obviously have similar work interests, it stands to reason that you might share other mutually rewarding interests in hobbies, sports, movies, and the like. You might even have a group of friends to which you both belong, and perhaps you all go out together after work. One thing leads to another, and you find yourself in an office romance.

While we highly recommend not getting involved romantically at work, it would be wrong to say that everything is negative about a workplace romance. Because you work with the person, you can observe his or her behaviors frequently and determine if this person is a good match for you. You could have the opportunity to go to lunch or work out together in the company exercise facility. You can get an idea if this person is a good love interest or simply a wolf in sheep's clothing.

You need to maintain a good balance between romance and work. Review the pointers in Figure 9.13 that might help you as you deal with office relationships.

While office romances may bring happiness, they have the potential to bring just as much sadness and anger, and at the same time, damage your career. Try very hard to avoid compromising situations. Proceed with caution, maturity, and wisdom.

> There is no greater hatred than the hatred between two people who once loved.
>
> —Sophocles

Figure 9.13 Tips for Managing Workplace Relationships

- Never have a relationship with your boss or a subordinate! You increase the risk of a sexual harassment lawsuit, you damage morale in the office, and you might get accused of preferential treatment. If you are a colleague competing for promotions, salaries, and other perks, naturally, people will say that you get better treatment. Managers tend to lose respect if they are caught dallying around with a subordinate. What about evaluations? How can a boss be unbiased in evaluating a love interest? "Just don't date anyone in your direct chain of command. Just don't do it," according to Taylor (2005).

- Never get involved with a married person—at work or anywhere else. You will quickly ruin your reputation. If this person will cheat on his or her spouse, he or she will cheat on you.

- If you sense that a work relationship is getting too serious, spend less time working and more time doing things that take your mind off this person. Go to places where you might meet someone with similar interests; spend more time working out; look up old friends.

- If you fall in love and you think you absolutely must have this person, one of you needs to move to another department or even to another company. Is this person worth giving up your job?

- If you become involved with a colleague, move very slowly into a serious relationship. It takes very mature people to handle a romantic relationship in the office.

- Kersten (2002) offers good advice: "Once you enter into a relationship, there are two people contributing to the way you are perceived in the company. It doesn't matter if you're being professional, if that other person is not, it's still going to impact you." What if your love interest shares intimate information with a colleague and it gets out around the watercooler?

- Do your homework. Does your company forbid interoffice dating? Are there unwritten rules that everyone seems to follow? What is the policy on harassment? Does your relationship with this person pose situations that may be harmful to the company? Are there any older, long-term employees in relationships with colleagues? Do you have very conservative bosses? Are other peers dating, and how has this affected their standing with their colleagues and bosses? If you were discussed in the same way as they are, could you live with it? How would you feel toward your romantic interest if the relationship cost you a promotion or your job?

- If you do get involved, make some hard-and-fast rules that you both will follow. No contact at work, no discussion of dating, no physical contact, and no talk of love. Perhaps the most important rule to agree on is this one: How will you treat each other if the relationship doesn't work out? Of course, there is no guarantee that either of you will live up to these promises. Can you be sure of what will happen if things don't turn out well? In extreme cases, one person or the other can't turn loose of their love interest, and it creates a bad scene at work, even resulting in violence and loss of job.

- Don't fall in love, get all starry-eyed, and stop paying attention to your job. You need to go to work, be prompt, meet deadlines, and handle your assignments in an excellent manner so your work doesn't suffer. Avoid e-mailing on company computers, and don't spend lots of time text-messaging when you should be working. Your computer at work belongs to the company, and anything you write can be examined by someone above your head if he or she chooses to do so. If this prince or princess doesn't work out, you still need your job and your reputation.

- If you break up—and you most likely will, according to statistics—handle it with maturity. Don't say bad things about your love interest; don't jump into another relationship at work or anywhere else right away; cool off. No one gets over a broken heart easily, but this is one of those times when you must deal with it in a very mature manner.

DON'T PARTY AT THE COMPANY PARTY

Is It Really Worth Ruining Your Professional Reputation?

The company party is not the place to party! You should be seen, be sociable, and be gone. You should arrive a little late and leave a little early. If everyone else is staying very late and drinking too much, this is a good reason for you to excuse yourself and leave. You should never have more than one drink at a company function. Nurse that drink as long as you are there, and refrain

Figure 9.14 How to Work a Room Like a Pro

- Survey the room before you enter to get "the lay of the land."

- If you have a drink, hold it in your left hand so your right hand is free to shake hands. Don't have more than one drink!

- Avoid eating. It is difficult to talk, eat, balance a plate, and shake hands. Eat before you go! You are there to do business, not eat. The worst thing you can do is to load up your plate and act like this is your last meal.

- Don't cluster in the corner with the only person you know! Move around the room, shaking hands and introducing yourself. Take the initiative. Most people will be glad you did.

- Focus on the other person. Smile and be friendly. Talk for a few minutes and move on.

- Sell yourself with a sound bite—something interesting about yourself. For example: "I'm John Martin, the new admissions coordinator at Marion Hospital."

- Don't look around the room or over the other person's shoulder while you're talking to someone. Look at the person as though he or she is the most interesting person in the room. Use the person's name.

- Don't talk about politics, make fun of a state, or tell religious or ethnic jokes. You never know whom you might offend.

- Don't talk about your health. People find this very boring. No one wants to hear about your operation or extensive details about your vacation.

- Converse a few minutes, excuse yourself, and move on. The idea is to meet people and network.

from drinking simply because the liquor is free. This is not the place for you to have too much to drink and make a fool of yourself. You don't have to drink more than anyone else just because the drinks are free.

Wear something that is in good taste. This is a work function—not a laid-back social gathering with your best buddies. Women certainly want to look attractive, but not overly sexy. Women in upper management are not likely to dress in skimpy, tight clothes. You want to fit in with them. Men should also dress like the company executives do. They won't have on jeans and t-shirts.

At every party there are two kinds of people—those who want to go home and those who don't. Trouble usually follows those who don't.

—Unknown

If you are attending a pool party, don't swim. You will look like a drowned rat while everyone else is still fresh and attractive. Don't parade around in a swimsuit even if you look like a movie star. Neither men nor women will win friends by insisting on showing off a great body. This is not the place!

How to Work a Room

As a businessperson, you probably will attend cocktail parties. You should consider them an extension of work. You are there to make contacts, make a good impression, network, expand your client base, and generally represent your company in a positive manner. In other words, you should work the room. Consider the basic tips in Figure 6.2 for working a room.

Business parties, receptions, and cocktail parties should be treated as an extension of work. You should look your best, present yourself well, and consider these events as a great opportunity to network.

ALCOHOL AND SUBSTANCE ABUSE

What Is the Cost to Companies and Individuals?

Alcohol and substance abuse by employees creates expensive problems for business and industry, including injuries on the job, increased premiums for health insurance, and missed work that affects others' jobs. "The loss to companies in the United States due to alcohol and drug-related abuse by employees totals $100 billion a year, according to the the National Clearinghouse for Alcohol and Drug Information (NCADI). These staggering numbers do not include the cost of diverting company resources that could be used for other purposes, toward addressing substance abuse issues. Nor does it include the 'pain and suffering' aspects, which cannot be measured in economic terms" (Buddy, 2011). Costs add up quickly in terms of expense of absenteeism, injuries, health insurance claims, loss of productivity, employee morale, theft, and fatalities.

According to NCADI statistics alcohol and drug users:

- Are far less productive.
- Use three times as many sick days.
- Are more likely to injure themselves or someone else.
- Are five times more likely to file worker's compensation claims.

One survey found that nine percent of heavy drinkers and 10 percent of drug users had missed work because of a

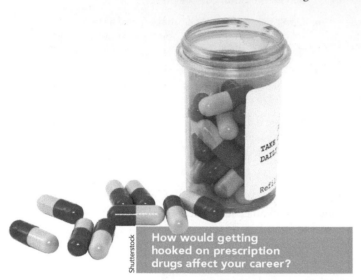

How would getting hooked on prescription drugs affect your career?

Shutterstock

Figure 9.15 Signs of Substance Abuse

- Showing a decline in grades or work performance
- Using room deodorizers and incense to hide odors
- Using drug paraphernalia such as baggies, pipes, or rolling paper
- Giving up hobbies and sports that he or she used to enjoy
- Getting drunk or high on a regular basis
- Lying about how much he or she is consuming
- Appearing rundown, hopeless, depressed, or suicidal
- Driving while under the influence of alcohol
- Avoiding friends and family to get drunk
- Hiding alcohol or drinking alone
- Becoming aggressive or hostile
- Getting suspended from school or work because of substance abuse–related incidents
- Getting in trouble with the police

Source: Adapted from Daly and Richards, 2007.

hangover, six percent had gone to work high or drunk in the past year, and 11 percent of heavy drinkers and 18 percent of drug users had skipped work in the past month. (Buddy, 2011)

There is no doubt that alcohol and substance abuse create serious problems at work and can cause you to lose your job. You are urged to use good judgment related to any type of substance abuse for your health, as well as your career.

People abuse substances such as drugs, tobacco, and alcohol for many complex reasons, but our society pays a terrible price because of these abuses. People harm themselves and others, work suffers, families are adversely affected, relationships are ruined, and many people end up in prison due to substance abuse. There is a strong correlation between drug dependence and crime. While the use of cocaine has declined, use of other drugs such as heroin and "club drugs" has increased (Daly & Richards, 2007).

> The estimated number of users of illicit drugs in the United States is about 13 million. About 10% of the population is dependent on alcohol and 25% of Americans smoke cigarettes.
> —National Household Survey

Friends, family, and coworkers may see some of the signs of substance abuse in people they know and care about listed in Figure 9.15.

While we cannot go into great depth on the issue of substance abuse here, suffice it to say that it is an increasingly serious problem among U.S. workers, and many people are not well-educated on the potential harmful effects of substance abuse. Many people, for example, have the mistaken idea that marijuana is harmless and non-habit-forming. According to Hoffman and Froemke (2007), "The odds of marijuana dependence in adulthood are six times higher for those who start using pot before the age of 15 than for those who begin after 18." Residual damage from substance abuse includes unwanted pregnancies, sexually transmitted diseases, and driving fatalities and accidents.

Binge drinking is drinking for the primary purpose of getting drunk. Cooper (2002) reported that 61 percent of men who binge drink practice unprotected sex, as compared to only 23 percent who do not binge drink. Forty-eight percent of women who participate in binge drinking practice unprotected sex, compared to 8 percent of women who do not practice binge drinking.

A substance abuse dependency started in college is very likely to carry over into the workplace. Many companies today will require a drug test before they will hire you. We offer the concerned advice of being very careful not to develop a substance abuse problem that can affect you for the rest of your life. If you have a problem or know of someone who does, get help at your earliest convenience.

> Eighty-five percent of the U.S. prison population either meets the medical criteria for substance abuse or addiction, or had histories of substance abuse; were under the influence of alcohol or other drugs at the time of their crime; committed their offense to get money to buy drugs; were incarcerated for an alcohol or drug law violation; or shared some combination of these characteristics.
> —"Behind Bars II: Substance Abuse and America's Prison Population"

Topic #1: How would you effectively handle someone who constantly gossips to you about your boss and co-workers?

Your thoughts on this topic:

Topic #2: How can you control sexual harassment in the workplace?

Your thoughts on this topic:

Topic #3: What should you do if your boss indicates that he or she is interested in a romantic liaison?

Your thoughts on this topic:

Print Name:_____

Topic #4: What is appropriate behavior at a company cocktail party?

Your thoughts on this topic:

Topic #5: What should you do if the company party evolves into a scene that you feel is inappropriate?

Your thoughts on this topic:

Topic #6: How does one avoid procrastination?

Your thoughts on this topic:

Print Name:_____

Topic #7: What strategies can you use to eliminate common distractions and interruptions while working?

Your thoughts on this topic:

Topic #8: Why is it imperative that you never speak negatively about your former OR current employer?

Your thoughts on this topic:

Topic #9: What is the significance of workplace politics? What is "fair play" in the workplace?

Your thoughts on this topic:

Print Name:_____

Topic #10 Are workplace romances dangerous and potentially unhealthy to your career?

Your thoughts on this topic:

Topic #11: How could your use of social media negatively affect your career?

Your thoughts on this topic:

Topic #12: How do "Mobile Manners" reflect on your level of professionalism?

Your thoughts on this topic:

Print Name:_____

Topic #13: What are the dangers of substance abuse to your career?
Your thoughts on this topic:

Topic #14: How do you make "the boss" look good and why is that important?
Your thoughts on this topic:

Topic #15: Why is it important to know how to "stand out" at a company meeting?
Your thoughts on this topic:

Topic #16: Why is it important to know how to grow from negative feedback?
Your thoughts on this topic:

Print Name:_____

Topic #17: How does one deal with a co-worker who constantly uses bad manners and makes inappropriate comments?

Your thoughts on this topic:

Topic #18: In what ways can we show appreciation and respect for people from different cultures?

Your thoughts on this topic:

Topic #19: Could your off-duty conduct have an effect on you professionally?

Your thoughts on this topic:

Print Name:_____

chapter ten

SERVE

MAXIMIZING CUSTOMER SERVICE AND PRODUCTIVITY IN THE WORKPLACE

The goal as a company is to have customer service that is not just the best, but legendary.
—Sam Walton, founder of Walmart

THE IMPORTANCE OF CUSTOMER SERVICE

How Do You Put the "WOW" Factor in Customer Service?

Most jobs today are service centered. Since the mid-fifties, the U.S. economy has gradually shifted from a manufacturing economy to a service economy, making customer service extremely important to all businesses and all employees.

All successful businesspeople understand a simple fact: Providing excellent customer service is absolutely essential to building a thriving business, whether it be health care, public safety, or solar technology! Customer service is about being so good at taking care of customers that they want to come back to your business. The definition of excellent customer service in a nutshell is this: Bring the customers back for more, and do what it takes to send them away happy. It sounds simple, but it takes dedicated, caring employees to make excellent customer service happen. As an employee, you want to be so good at taking care of customers that you personally are known for putting the "WOW" factor in customer service. You do this by carefully paying attention to your customers; listen to what they are saying, and they will tell you what they need to be happy. Good customer service is essentially all about building relationships.

To be successful in providing excellent customer service, a company must make a commitment to relentlessly pursue a system that exceeds customers' expectations. The customer service philosophy of a company must include all aspects of the **service triangle** (see Figure 10.1), as defined by Albrecht and Zemke (2001). According to these authors, every company should have a **service strategy** that distinguishes it from the competition. Most companies delivering the same services and products have only one way to distinguish themselves—service. Further, Albrecht and Zemke state that companies should have **service systems.** Systems are the points at which services actually get delivered. It could be the telephone, a drive-through window, an ATM, or a face-to-face meeting with a front-line employee. The mistake that companies make, according to Albrecht and Zemke (2001), is that they make systems convenient for themselves and forget about their customers.

Finally, companies should focus on **the people.** The people are the deliverers of service, the ones who make or break a company's reputation. The hard part about the people component of the service triangle is that this group is usually the lowest paid and often the least trained group in most companies. The people are also the most important part of the service triangle. "Companies that have earned a reputation for service excellence understand the employees interacting with customers every day are the true ambassadors of their brands. As a result, finding the right people and putting them in a position to succeed is key" (Business Wire News Releases, 2011).

"Our primary focus is on hiring the right people and just letting them be themselves," states Aaron Magness, senior director of brand marketing and business development at Zappos.com. "You can't hire someone and teach them to provide great customer service, but you can hire people who are committed to providing great customer service" (Business Wire News Releases, 2011). All employees—top to bottom—must be so well-trained that customer service is on their minds at all times.

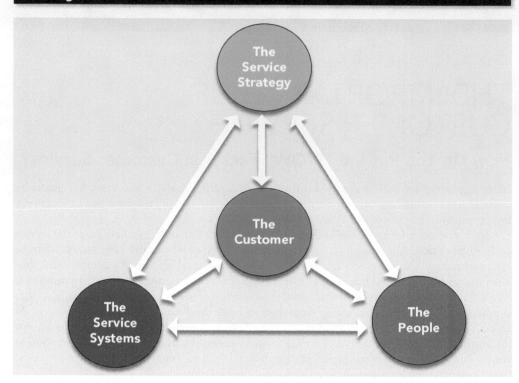

Figure 10.1 Service Triangle

How Do Customers Judge Customer Service?

"Getting service right is more than just a nice thing to do; it's a must do," said Jim Bush, Executive Vice President, World Service for American Express (Business Wire News Releases, 2011). Although nine in ten Americans (91%) consider the level of customer service important when deciding to do business with a company, only 24 percent believe companies value their business and will work hard to keep it. Most feel businesses could do much more to keep them as customers.

According to the American Express Global Customer Service Barometer (2011), a majority of Americans report that quality customer service is more important to them in today's economic environment (61%). Seventy percent will spend an average of 13 percent more when they believe a company provides excellent service. However, it appears that many companies are not paying attention to their customers' needs, because six in ten customers feel companies are helpful but don't do anything extra to keep their business. Twenty-six percent feel companies are actually doing less to keep their business than they did the previous year.

- 21% believe that companies take their business for granted.
- 27% feel businesses have not changed their attitude toward customer service.
- 28% say that companies are now paying *less* attention to good service.

This report does not bode well for U.S. businesses.

> *American consumers are willing to spend more with companies that provide outstanding service. They will tell, on average, twice as many people about bad service than they will about good service. Ultimately, great service can drive sales and customer loyalty.*
>
> *—Jim Bush, executive VP for American Express*

The same study conducted by American Express revealed that customers use the following criteria when making a buying decision:

- Value for the price
- Overall quality of customer service
- Knowing the company will be there to resolve any problems
- Benefits the product or service provides
- Convenience
- The way the product or service makes them feel

"Customers appear to think that the three most influential factors when deciding which companies they do business with include personal experience (98%), a company's reputation or brand (92%), and recommendations from friends and family (88%)" (Miller, 2010).

© Shutterstock

What would you say to a customer to make her feel that you care about her personally?

Customer Service Is All about Relationships

So how do you go about building good relationships? You do what you say you are going to do no matter how difficult it is. You don't make promises you can't deliver. It is often said, "Under promise, over deliver." In other words, do more than you said you would do, and people will not only be pleased, they will be amazed. Even more important, they will tell other people. The best advertisement is a satisfied customer who can't wait to tell someone how good your service is and how much he or she likes you personally.

One of the best ways to build relationships is to learn people's names and use them. Say things like, "Welcome back, Mrs. Smith. We are happy to have you with us again today. How can I help you?" Later, during the conversation, you might ask a question about someone in her family that she has mentioned to you. "How is your daughter doing in college?" Or "How is that adorable little granddaughter who was with you last time?" By all means, be sincere. Nothing is worse than false compliments or pretending to be interested. Customers value sincerity.

GRADUATE Quote

Erica R. Harrison
Graduate!
Lincoln College of Technology, Cincinnati, OH
Career: Medical Administrative Assistant,
 Pediatric Associates of Fairfield

The most important advice that I can give you is to believe in yourself. I know that sounds trivial, but it is vitally important. You have to believe that your degree and experience will provide you with a better life. You can't sit around waiting for the future to get better, for someone to wave a magical wand and give you your dream job. You have to make your own future. Your training and degree are the first steps in making your own future. Use them and never look back.

> *In the United States, 74 percent of the gross domestic product and 79 percent of jobs are derived from the performance of services rather than the production of jobs.*
> —Karl Albrecht and Ron Zemke

Some of the best people at handling customer service actually keep a file on their best customers. After they leave, they write information to use when calling them on the telephone or when greeting them in the business. For example, Mr. Aamann might have mentioned to you that his son is in the Navy SEALs. You can inquire about his son and how he is doing. You can't possibly keep all this information in your head, so you need to make notes about pertinent facts. A simple index card file can be used, or you may use a computer program such as Microsoft Office vCards or create a customer service database using software such as FileMaker.

There are many definitions of customer service. Some excellent definitions follow:

- Doing ordinary things extraordinarily well
- Going beyond what is expected
- Adding value and integrity to every action
- Being at your best with every customer
- Discovering new ways to delight those you serve
- Surprising yourself with how much you can do
- Taking care of your customer like you would take care of your grandmother (Carlaw, 1999, p. 4)

Study the points about excellent customer service in Figure 10.2. Then consider customers' wants in Figure 10.3 as you think about excellent customer service.

Figure 10.2 · Top 10 Customer Service Commandments

1. Implement a customer service plan, and be sure every employee has been properly educated in how to deliver outstanding service. Everyone in the company should understand the first rule of doing business: The customer is the boss. All employees need to grasp the fact that customers pay their salaries and without them, there will be no jobs. Good customer service is added value for your business. The best customer service is delivered *before* the customer even knows there is a problem. All employees should be so attuned to solving problems that they are alert and take care of problems before they magnify. One bad apple can mess up things for a lot of others. Unhappy customers are said to tell at least 18 other people about their bad experience.

Employees should never discuss their political or religious views with customers. You have no idea what individual customers believe, and you can offend them without even knowing you have done so.

2. Answer the telephone on the first ring if possible. The phone should never ring more than three or four times before someone answers it. *Someone*—not an answering machine! Nothing is more frustrating than getting a long list of connection possibilities that lead to another long list of possibilities, none of which answers the question that you need answered, especially if you are in a hurry. Answer politely, completely, and with a smile in your voice. When you are talking on the telephone, all you have to use to communicate are your tone of voice and your words. So smile, literally, and it will come across in your voice. Never put anyone on hold unless you absolutely have to. Then ask the person if he or she minds being put on hold. Say something like this: "Would you mind holding for just a moment, please?" Then get back to the person as quickly as you can. Time passes very slowly when waiting.

3. Know the answers to the most frequently asked questions. Every employee should know the answers to the top 25 questions that customers are likely to ask. If you don't know the answer, respond politely, "I don't know, but I will find out, and I will call you back immediately." Then do exactly what you said you would do. Go find out and call the customer back immediately.

4. Keep your promises. If you tell the customer her new carpet will be installed on Monday, she is going to be expecting you to deliver. And if you don't, she is going to be upset. Not only will she be upset, she will tell everyone with whom she comes in contact that day and every day until you install the carpet. One unhappy customer can cause you a world of hurt! If you think you might need until Tuesday, schedule her for Tuesday. If you are able to install the carpet on Monday, call her and give her that option. Chances are, the customer will be happy and impressed. You have under promised and over delivered.

5. Listen to what your customers are saying. Listen, listen, listen! So many employees don't pay any attention to what the customer is telling them. Then they have to ask again or they get the order wrong. Look at your customer; nod to indicate that you are hearing what he or she is saying; take notes so you don't forget; ask questions so you get the order right. Make customers feel good about being your customer by doing things that let them know that they are valued and appreciated. If you are taking the customer to be helped by someone in another department, introduce him or her; "Jack, this is Mr. Redmond. He is one of our favorite long-term customers. Please take good care of him."

6. Handle complaints quickly and carefully. This is called "damage control," and if it is done properly, it can keep customers for life. Conversely, it can lose customers forever. People who are unhappy are going to complain. They will complain to the company, and they will complain to anyone else who will listen. This is known as the *multiplier effect.* Consumers who are unhappy about their customer service experience will tell twice as many people (18 or more) as they do about a good experience (9 people). "Customers who have a fantastic service experience say friendly representatives (65%) who are ultimately able to solve their concerns (66%) are most influential" (Business Wire News Releases, 2011). Every interaction with customers is crucially important to a company.

First of all, thank the person for bringing the complaint to you so that you can solve it. Do not argue with the customer and say that he or she is wrong. Apologize for the inconvenience, and explain how you are going to take care of the problem. How can you solve the problem so the customer leaves happy and loyal even though he or she has been inconvenienced? If you don't act like you care, no solution will make the person happy.

Try to find ways to say "yes." Naturally, you can't give away the store, and you have to make a profit, but you can find other ways to say "yes." If you can't negotiate on the price of a big-ticket item, for example, you can throw in a few inexpensive extras that make the customer feel like you cared and that you tried to make him or her happy. If the customer has had a bad experience, what can you do to make up for it? Can you give him or her a coupon? Can you add some small item to the order to show that you are sincere?

When you have finished, thank the customer again for letting you know about the unsatisfactory experience. Say something like this, "Once again, I am so sorry you had this problem. This is not like us because we strive to be 100 percent correct all the time. We appreciate your

helping us get better." Remember, you want customers to come back. You cannot build a business on one-time customers, especially if they go away unhappy. You want customers who are so loyal that they stick with you for a lifetime. Excellent service builds this kind of business and attracts this kind of customer.

7. If someone has a problem that you can solve easily, do it, do it now, and do it for free. Maybe a customer needs a copy made or some simple solution. Just do it for the customer and smile while you are helping him or her. You may not make any money from that customer today, but who knows how much he or she might spend during the next visit to your business. Say something like, "It is my pleasure." Little things bring big results.

8. Give more than is expected by going the extra mile. Go out of your way to be helpful. Don't point to where an item or a person is. Get up and go with the customer to the right place. Everyone is in a hurry, and this will let your customer know that you care enough to be helpful. Because the future of all companies lies in keeping customers happy, think of ways to elevate yourself above the competition. Consider the following:

- What can you give customers that they cannot get elsewhere?

- What can you do to follow-up and thank people even when they don't buy?

- What can you give customers that is totally unexpected? (Friedman, 2011).

9. Try to establish a pleasant environment throughout the business. Today's employees are overworked, overstressed, and sometimes underpaid, so it is difficult to get excellent customer service from everyone. Although establishing an excellent work environment where internal customers (employees) feel valued has to come from the top, you can do your part by coming to work with a great attitude and doing everything you can to be supportive of your colleagues. Leave your personal problems at home—no one really wants to hear whiners and complainers. Bring your "I feel great" attitude to work and share it with everyone. In the long run, excellent customer service on your part will pay off because some satisfied customers will tell your boss how much they appreciate you.

10. Know your business. Customers want to feel like they are talking to someone who knows what he or she is talking about and can answer questions about the products. For example, if a customer asks you a question about a computer, he or she expects you to know the answer. If you can't answer questions about your products or services, the customer will lose interest and go somewhere else. Learn everything you can about your job. Then learn everything you can about the rest of the company. The more you know, the more likely you are to get promoted.

Figure 10.3 What Customers Want/What Customers Don't Want

What Customers Want	What Customers Don't Want
They want you to smile when you greet them.	They don't want you to use company jargon that they don't understand.
They want fast, courteous service, and they want you to acknowledge them and let them know you see them waiting.	They don't want to stand in long lines without being acknowledged while employees act oblivious.
They want you to know their names and use them.	They don't like loud music, horseplay, gum chewing, and personal conversations that have nothing to do with business.
They want you to know your products.	They don't like phones that are not answered promptly or being put on hold.
They want good, competitive products and services.	They don't like flippant, disrespectful attitudes.
They want employees who demonstrate initiative and make things happen.	They don't like employees who can't work one minute past quitting time to finish up their business and take their money.
They want to be respected.	They don't like negativism between employees.
They want you to treat them like they are somebody.	They don't want to hear about your grandchildren, gallbladder surgery, or vacation—but they want to tell you about theirs.
They want you to listen and solve their problem.	They don't like rude, inattentive employees when they have a problem.
They want you to stay cool, even when they lose theirs.	They don't want you to promise what you can't deliver.
They want effective follow-up.	They don't want you to forget to call them as you promised.
They want to do business with a company that has a progressive, successful image.	They don't like employees who bad-mouth their own business or their boss.
They want you to act like you are interested in taking their money and that you understand that their money pays your salary.	They don't like for you to keep working and not stop and look up at them. They want you to give them your undivided attention.
They want you to smile and thank them.	They don't like for you to take their money and not thank them.

DEALING WITH DIFFICULT CUSTOMERS

How Do You Manage Challenging Situations?

Some people are just naturally difficult, but most people are reasonable if you listen to them and try to understand them. People who lose their temper might just hang up on you, or they might ask to speak to your supervisor. Many will threaten to switch their business to a competitor. If you are on the receiving end of an irate customer's anger, it can be unpleasant, but there are ways to handle this kind of customer and, in most cases, turn a bad situation into a good one. Some tips on dealing with difficult people follow:

> *Success is never final.*
> —*Winston Churchill*

- **Even if the customer is wrong, make up your mind not to argue.** Stay calm and relatively quiet. Be patient and let him or her vent. You can't fight fire with fire! You'll both get burned!

- **Listen to what the irate customer is saying.** Stay calm and try to uncover why he or she is upset. There may be a legitimate complaint that someone needs to hear and correct.

- **Watch your body language as well as the customer's.** If the customer indicates that he or she is getting out of control, excuse yourself and give the individual time to get control. Get assistance if you think you need it.

- **Do not take the customer's anger personally.** Chances are good that the person is just having a bad day, and you are an easy target. If you stay calm and demonstrate sincere concern, the other person will typically calm down and might even apologize. But if you meet anger with anger, the situation will escalate into an unpleasant situation.

- **If the customer appears to be capable of violence, excuse yourself and get a supervisor.** You want to solve as many problems personally as you can, but occasionally it is best to ask for help. You do not have to take unwarranted abuse. Cursing, yelling, threatening, and other forms of aggressiveness do not have to be tolerated. Walk away.

- **Use calming phrases** such as, "I understand, Mrs. Jenkins. You have a right to be upset. This is not like our company, so please give me a chance to get this corrected. Why don't you have a cup of coffee and give me a few minutes to solve this problem?"

- **Solve the problem and do so immediately if you can.** If the person has been dishonest or has damaged the product, you may want to discuss the matter with your supervisor before providing an answer. If there is no reason for you not to take care of the problem, get it done as urgently as you can.

- **Learn your company's policies and procedures.** You cannot do anything that your company's policies don't allow you to do. Some customers don't want to hear this and will tell you, "I don't care about your policies. This television isn't any good, and I want my money back." Some will say things like this after they have used an item well beyond the warranty. Many are just fishing and hoping you will give them a new item even though they know the warranty has expired. Depending on company policy and your supervisor's decision, you may be able to offer the customer a good discount on a new item or make some other concession that might make him or her happy.

- **Strive to build a good relationship with every customer, even the difficult ones.** It may take time, but you can usually win over most people. Give it your best shot; make it your mission to get this person on your side and turn him or her into a dedicated, loyal, lifelong customer. There will be days when you have to face an irate person face-to-face or on the telephone. Try to remain calm, use a soothing voice, give the person a chance to vent, and do everything you can to solve the problem in a satisfactory manner. The goal is to keep the customer and to turn him or her into a nicer person.

© Alamy

How would you diffuse a customer's anger?

BIGGEST INTERVIEW *Blunders*

Jeremy had an appointment to interview with a major company as a customer service representative. When asked how he would handle a customer who grew angry and yelled at him on the telephone and demanded that he refund his money, Jeremy replied, "I wouldn't take his abuse. I'd tell him to take his business elsewhere and then I'd slam the phone down." Needless to say, Jeremy did not get this job.

LESSON: Unless a customer is extremely abusive, you should consider the customer to always be right. You are trying to build repeat business, so you need to try to find a solution to the customer's complaint.

CUSTOMER SERVICE FOR ELECTRONIC AND MOBILE COMMERCE

What Are the Advantages and Disadvantages?

Information technology and communications technologies have converged to create e-commerce, bringing advantages and disadvantages for consumers and businesspeople alike. One thing is certain, however—businesses must have a web presence today, and many have only a web presence. Some people refer to companies who have both physical plants and a

Figure 10.4 **Advantages and Disadvantages of E-Commerce as It Relates to Customer Service**

Advantages of E-Commerce as It Relates to Customer Service	Disadvantages of E-Commerce as It Relates to Customer Service
Business can be conducted 24/7; the physical storefront does not have to be open to do business.	Someone has to be paying attention 24/7 for technological problems or customers' questions.
The business can market worldwide and have access to a global marketplace.	Worldwide communications often come with language barriers and shipping costs and problems.
Catalogs, ads, and brochures can be delivered instantly.	Because speed of delivery is instant, customers expect quick responses.
The business can use customer outsourcing (meaning that many of the tasks typically performed by employees are done by customers) and shift some of the costs to the customers.	Many customers need assistance and they expect it immediately.
Customers can pay online, and the business can have instant access to their funds.	Paying online is troublesome to some customers, and they may decide not to buy because they are concerned about having their identities stolen or credit cards abused.
Nonperishable goods can be sold directly to the consumer.	Perishable goods often cannot be satisfactorily shipped and leaves room for problems and complaints.
A website provides some very good sensory information for sight and auditory.	A website cannot provide certain sensory information such as smell or weight, and the consumer may not be able to see the item from all angles.
Customers can buy products without having to go to a brick-and-mortar facility.	Customers have to wait for their products and cannot take them home immediately.
People are beginning to trust online businesses as orders have increased dramatically.	Returning goods can be a problem: customers are not sure if products will reach the source, don't want to pay return shipping, or are concerned about getting credit for returned goods.
A customer service phone number can be posted so customers can reach a live person to answer questions.	The business is not conducive for very large or very small orders because of shipping costs, especially overseas.
The business can respond by phone or e-mail to customers' questions and do so immediately.	Customers may not be sure if the business is legitimate or is some kind of bogus operation that might take their money and deliver no goods.

web presence as using "clicks and mortar." Your first job might very well be working with a web-based company, especially if you are good with technology. Although customer service may be delivered differently, it is still just as important. In fact, delivering excellent customer service via the Internet might be even more important, because chances are almost 100 percent that you will never see or talk to your customer.

Consider the advantages and disadvantages of customer service delivered electronically that are detailed in Figure 10.4.

> *Friends do business with friends.*
> *—J. W. Marriott*

PUTTING IT ALL TOGETHER

The information contained here is very important to your success as a professional. No business can function without customers, and the best way to attract and retain customers is to provide excellent customer service. One way for you to gain positive attention from your supervisors is to take care of your company's customers, because many of them will tell your boss how you went out of your way to help them.

Understanding your company's organizational structure, the top management's strategy and vision, and the lines of authority as they affect your job gives you an advantage over those who don't take time to become informed. You can never know too much about your company and its directions!

DIGITAL BRIEFCASE

EXPLORING ONLINE CUSTOMER SERVICE TECHNIQUES

E-mail at least five of your friends on Facebook and have them send you one customer service mistake or offense that they have personally encountered in the past few months. Select five complaints from the complete list and develop a customer service technique to respond to each problem. Format your list and solutions in a Word chart and send it to your Facebook friends who helped you with the list.

Customer service techniques are somewhat different for online companies as compared to storefront businesses, but they are still vitally important. In fact, they may be even more important because the customer is interacting via computer rather than face to face. When customers walk into a small specialty store in a mall, usually someone greets them. When customers access an online business, they usually have one or two ways to get information about products and to have their questions answered: an online chat, in which both parties type their questions and answers, and a video chat, in which a live person answers questions and shows you products if you desire.

Go online to the Lands' End website (www.landsend.com) and Amazon's Help page (www.amazon.com/gp/help/customer/display.html?ref= gwmbhe?ie=UTF8&nodeId=508510) and explore how they interact with their online customers. You might try accessing each type of service and asking a question to determine how satisfactory each type of service is. After you have examined both live video chat and online service, make a chart that details the advantages and disadvantages of each type of service.

> *Sixty eight percent of customers quit shopping at a business because they are dissatisfied with the attitude of a company employee.*
> *—U.S. Small Business Administration and U. S. Chamber of Commerce*

REFERENCES

Albrecht, K., & Zemke, R. (2001). *Service America in the new economy.* New York: McGraw-Hill.

American Express Global Customer Service Barometer. (2011). Market comparison of findings. Retrieved April 24, 2011, from http://about.americanexpress.com/news/docs/2011x/AXP_2011_csbar_market.pdf

Business Wire News Releases. (2011). Good service is good business: American consumers willing to spend more with companies that get service right, according to American Express Survey. Retrieved May 8, 2011, from http://finance.boston.com/boston/news/read?GUID=18338537.

Carlaw, P. (1999). *Big book of customer service training games.* New York: McGraw-Hill.

Fontaine. C. W. (2007). Organizational structure: A critical factor for organizational effectiveness and employee satisfaction. White paper. Northeastern University.

Friedman, S. (2011). The ten commandments of great customer service. Retrieved May 8, 2011, from http://marketing.about.com/od/relationshipmarketing/a/crmtopten.htm.

Management Study Guide, Columbia College. (2010). Levels of management. Retrieved on May 9, 2010, from www.managementstudyguide.com/managementlevels.htm.

Miller, R. (2010). Do companies really value their customers? Retrieved May 8, 2010, from http://customerservicezone.com/cgi-bin/links/jump.cgi?ID=1284.